So Far So Great !

So Far So Great !

LESSONS LEARNED FROM AN
AUTISTIC SON'S JOURNEY
FROM INFANCY TO MIDDLE AGE

By

MARY P. MILLER

TRAP DOCK PRESS

ISBN: 978 0-692-59120-8

Printed in the United States of America

Dedication

For Betsy, Allison and Jay
my inspiration

Author's Note

Optimism is the faith that leads to achievement.
Nothing can be done without hope and confidence.
HELEN KELLER

When my son was two years old, I began to keep a journal, something I had never done before. I knew Jay was special, and I felt compelled to document his development. The traditional "baby book" format didn't quite cut it – small spaces to be filled in with first steps and first words were not adequate.

I needed pages and pages to describe and record the milestones and challenges in the life of a young child with autism, as well as space to accommodate my own thoughts and emotions. While the journal captures only five years of Jay's life, it provides the basis for a much larger story, our story, Jay's and mine. By the end it is a good story, but it was not an easy one.

My journal is not entirely balanced. In an entry from February 1973, when Jay was just three years old, I wrote, "I look at this diary as my hope book. As I read it over, I realize that I'm recording much more of the good than the bad. Maybe I'm afraid if I don't write down the good things when they happen, they will disappear – go away forever."

I needed to hold on tightly to progress, however small. Each baby step provided a springboard for the next, and often I had to will myself onward. But I hope I've described the challenges and heartbreaks honestly.

More importantly, I want to offer my readers not only lessons learned, but a sense of optimism, of what is possible, and through many tears, a sense of joy and hope for what can be.

Chapter 1

Within the Range of Normal

W hat's wrong with that kid anyway?" The words cut through the laughter and conversation at a family gathering on Cape Cod in August 1970. My husband's cousin cocked his head to one side as he stared at my eight month old son, as if a different angle would make sense of Jay's odd behavior. Tears burned behind my eyes. All the quiet worry I had stuffed deep down inside my gut came roaring to the surface. I had no answer to his question.

———

"You're the handsomest boy in the whole world," I'd told my baby son five months earlier. Adorable in his blue and white romper, he was ready to have his picture taken at a local studio. We put on a fashion show for his sisters. Four-year old Betsy and eighteen-month old Allison giggled and planted wet kisses all over his shiny clean face before we headed out to capture his image for posterity.

Jay was an easy baby. From day one, he slept through the night and was peaceful during the day. I was amazed and grateful throughout that winter because his sisters never stopped moving.

Allison, a happy, curious toddler, was a miniature Houdini. At sixteen months she had mastered the art of scaling the side of her crib and could open doors and cupboards more quietly than a thief. When the doorbell rang repeatedly one frigid January day, I found her on the doorstep wearing only a diaper and undershirt, holding the hand of a young hippie with a scraggly beard. "Is this yours?" he asked. With Jay in one arm, I knelt to scoop Allison into the other.

My voice trembled. "Where was she?"

"Just coming down the sidewalk," he answered.

Nothing, it seemed, could contain our chaos.

During that cold and snowy winter, it often seemed easier to stay inside than to bundle up three little ones to brave the outdoors. And since my husband Frank's new job took him on the road for days, sometimes weeks, adult company proved hard to come by. So when winter reluctantly gave way to spring, walks around the neighborhood became a regular ritual. Four-month old Jay rode in his carriage, his sisters dancing on either side, discovering plants pushing up through the fresh spring earth, chasing after birds and squirrels.

My friend Connie had just delivered her fifth baby, her first son. "Our boys will go to kindergarten together," she said.

"They'll be fast friends, best buddies," I replied. Life felt full.

But as April slipped into May, cracks began to mar this perfect picture. Certain things about Jay didn't seem right. Although grateful for his sound sleep every night, I began to worry that I just didn't hear him waken. For a few nights I slept in the extra bed in his room. He never made a peep.

"Is this normal?" I asked his doctor.

"Consider yourself lucky," he said.

He's right, I thought. I'm lucky.

But then there was Jay's eating. As a newborn he'd had trouble sucking. The nurses put preemie nipples on his bottles, but my big, full-term baby didn't take easily to those either. And months later when I tried to introduce food with texture, he rejected it. At first he made a funny face, but then he began to gag and choke on anything that wasn't pureed.

"He's such a good baby," I said to Frank one night when the house was quiet, "but I worry about his eating. Allie and Betsy weren't like this."

Frank wasn't a worrier. "It's just the way he's developing, Mary. Give it time."

The more I fretted, the more I found to fret about. When I held Jay, his body remained rigid. When distressed, he was impossible to console. When I tried to comfort him, he arched his back away from me and screamed.

"Please settle down baby," I'd murmur, then sing the lullaby I'd sung to the girls:

> *Rocking, rocking, rocking, rocking,*
> *Backward and forward, to and fro.*
> *Rocking, rocking, rocking, rocking,*
> *That's the way Jay likes to go.*

Nothing worked. My tears mingled with his.

I talked to Jay constantly during the day, just as I had with his sisters. They'd always follow me with their eyes and reward me with smiles. He simply lay quietly wherever I put him down and stared straight ahead.

"Please my sweet baby," I begged. "Look at me."

No response.

Several months later while walking Jay in his stroller, I ran into Connie with her infant son. Though months younger than Jay, he looked at me and smiled. Jay's eyes wandered without focus.

"He must be tired." Connie's gentle observation was made with great care, as if we both knew something wasn't right, but we wouldn't step into forbidden territory.

Family members noticed too. My husband's parents welcomed us for visits all summer long at their Chatham home on Cape Cod, a house often packed with three generations of fun and bedlam. It was there that Frank's cousin asked, "What's wrong with that kid anyway?"

"What's wrong with Jay?" I asked Frank. "What's wrong with *me*?"

He had no answers.

Jay was missing developmental milestones, but he was also acquiring peculiar behaviors. While other children his age reached out to grab things, Jay sat on the floor staring endlessly at a shadow. While other children played with toys and looked at books, Jay rocked ferociously to the steady hum of the dishwasher, flapping his hands wildly or flipping them in front of his eyes with his head cocked toward the light.

He wouldn't tolerate solid food nor could he drink from a cup. He didn't babble. Instead he hummed a sing-song monotone. As he approached his first birthday, he showed no inclination to walk or even crawl. Most alarming, he still wouldn't look at me.

Disinterested in people, Jay obsessed over cylindrical objects, mostly cans and containers that he collected and lined up in neat rows on the floor. Because he paid no attention to my voice, I worried he might be deaf, until I saw him turn toward the pop of a soda can being opened in another room of the house.

I couldn't worry alone anymore, so again I spoke to Jay's physician, a family practitioner. I had met him and his wife shortly after Frank and I moved from Boston to Greenfield, my hometown, where I was teaching kindergarten. The doctor's daughter, a joyful little girl who sailed through my class, had difficulties in first grade, and her parents came to me for counsel. He and his wife became friends, and Frank and I chose him as the physician for our first baby.

He'd been great with my girls, and I'd always felt comfortable sharing my concerns with him, so I peppered him with questions. "Why isn't Jay trying to crawl? His sisters did by this time."

"Girls tend to be ahead of boys at this age," he assured me.

"But why isn't he more responsive?"

"It's unfair to make comparisons. He's certainly within the range of normal."

The doctor's tone stung. Was I an overly anxious mother? I repeated the words "within the range of normal," wanting to believe them, hoping they would prove to be true. But more odd behaviors, unusual hand movements and sounds, were beginning to erode my hope.

LESSON 1

You know your child better than anyone.
Trust your instincts.

Chapter 2

The Unthinkable

amn it, Frank, what's going on?" Again I was looking for answers he didn't have.

Jay was sitting on the floor rocking and humming. Why wouldn't he look at me? Why was he so slow? Why did he have such strange mannerisms? Could he be retarded? Was his brain damaged?

Desperate for answers, I had no idea where to find them. There was no internet. Steve Jobs and Bill Gates were 15 years old and the information highway a fantasy. So I returned to the only resource I knew: Jay's doctor. He continued to reproach me for comparing Jay to his sisters, repeating, "within the range of normal."

His impatience was obvious, but I couldn't let go. Finally a small victory: undoubtedly tired of listening to me, he referred us to Dr. D, a pediatric neurologist at Massachusetts General Hospital in Boston.

I couldn't wait to get help for Jay, to make sense of this nightmare. I didn't trust the familiar voices around me anymore, but I also hadn't begun to accept the possibility of a lifetime disorder, something that wouldn't "go away." Our appointment was set for December 1970. Jay was one year old.

Easygoing, Dr. D was instantly likable. He gave me a sense of well-being as he observed Jay, talked to him and watched us interact with him. Jay sat on the floor rocking, flapping his hands in front of his eyes from time to time. When I picked him up, he sat contentedly on my lap, but didn't react to my voice with eye contact or sounds.

"Is something wrong with him?" I asked. "Is it a disease? Is he brain damaged?"

"No," Dr. D replied. "He exhibits symptoms of an early childhood syndrome, but we shouldn't be alarmed."

"Early childhood syndrome," I repeated. "What does that mean?"

Dr. D offered no clinical diagnosis, nor did he suggest any therapy or treatment. "Take him home and continue to do what you are doing, providing Jay with a caring, loving family environment. We'll meet again in six months."

While relieved that whatever was wrong wasn't a disease with a name, I was frustrated that this specialist had no explanation for Jay's behavior and slow development. Had I been familiar with the psychiatric terms used at the time, such as "childhood schizophrenia," I might have begun to piece things together by myself, but a psychiatric problem or mental illness of any kind wasn't on my radar.

I tried to quiet my worry. Even without concrete answers, I knew we were right to take Jay to Boston. Surely in time, with more visits, we'd get to the root of the problem, and Jay's development would improve.

I focused on the coming summer and how Jay would run around with his cousins on the Cape, how life would finally get easier: no more baby food jars or jump seats or other infant equipment to lug around. I thought about how he and Allison, only fifteen months apart, would become pals. I couldn't bear to think of Jay's life unfolding any other way.

But during the next six months the bizarre behaviors became worse. Late nights with Dr. Spock offered no solutions or comfort as they had with the girls' earaches, colic and other minor problems that keep young mothers awake at night.

Frank tried to comfort me, saying, "Things will be all right. Give it time." But I couldn't hold onto his words. I was no longer convinced he believed them himself.

My closest friends were patient and understanding. With no more knowledge than I had, they assured me that time would take care of things, whether they believed it or not.

Finally I began to search for information on my own. Our local library had no helpful textbooks, so I made the short drive to UMass Amherst, where I found books on child development and psychology written by people I'd never heard of. I carried them to a big table in the quiet room, and referenced Jay's symptoms. A world of dread began to unfold. At first I couldn't believe what I read, so I went to the next book, and then the next. The word AUTISM leapt from the pages.

Swiss psychiatrist Eugene Bueler coined the term "autism" in 1908 to refer to schizophrenic adults he described as self-isolated and self-absorbed. And Dr. Leo Kanner, a child psychiatrist at Johns Hopkins in Baltimore, wrote a paper in 1943 applying the term autism to children, calling the disorder Early Infantile Autism.

While Dr. Kanner believed autism had a biological basis, he believed the child's environment played a major role in the development of the disorder, specifically highly intelligent, cold obsessive parents. He coined the term "refrigerator mother," one who could neither nurture nor bond with her child. And in 1967 the famous Austrian-born child psychologist Bruno Bettelheim published <u>The Empty Fortress</u>, further promulgating the refrigerator mother theory.

The words described my son to a tee, words written by people who had never laid eyes on him. Was it possible? Was my child like the children described on these pages? Was my son autistic? Most terrifying, was it my fault? Was I a refrigerator mother?

"Early childhood syndrome," said Dr. D at Mass General. Was he alluding to Early Infantile Autism?

My heart was shattered. Jay was 18 months old. Frank was traveling, so I had to absorb the information alone.

After I put the children to bed that night, I poured a glass of wine and sat on our back porch in a wonderful old rocker, a chair that had always offered comfort. I cried as I had never cried in my life. I wanted to scream at God, tell Him how unfair He was. I was lost in fear, fear that I wouldn't be able to help my son. My world shifted on its axis forever.

Shaken to my core, I'd look at my beautiful children and murmur, "Am I cold? Not connecting? I could never hurt my babies. I'm a warm, loving mother."

But my reading had created doubts that attacked my common sense. Even though Bruno Bettelheim's research and many of his theories would eventually be rejected, he was leaving mothers like me staggering under a burden of guilt.

I'd have to dig deep to find the strength to help my son. I'd need support and guidance. But where would I find it?

When we met with Dr. D in June, I was ready to discuss autism. He listened to my findings and conclusions, jotting in Jay's folder now and then. But when I ran out of steam, Dr.

D would have none of it. "Let's not jump to conclusions," he cautioned.

"But could I have caused this problem?" Barely able to speak, I was terrified of the answer but desperate for a plan. I had to do the right thing for Jay.

"Mary," Dr. D replied, "you would be astounded at the resiliency of children found in unspeakable conditions. Resist the impulse to look inward. This is not about a mistreated child. Jay comes from a loving home."

I clung to his reassuring words, but still he offered no treatment or therapy. Again the same advice: "Go home and do what you have been doing, providing a loving home for Jay and his sisters."

Dr. D's sympathy and understanding bolstered me momentarily. I trusted him. I *needed* to trust him. But when we returned home, just opening the front door set me adrift. If I hadn't felt so vulnerable, so needy, so guilty, would I have been enraged by Dr. D's lack of prescription? Would I have pressed him for more answers?

Autism or not, Jay was not "within the range of normal." It was now painfully clear that he was lost. He was somewhere else. And I was frantic to find him.

How could I have foreseen this nightmare on that beautiful, snowy day in December, waiting for Jay to arrive?

Lᴇssᴏɴ 2

Don't get lost in denial.
It will cost you precious time.

Chapter 3

Joy

The snow started at dusk on December 18, tiny flakes that squeaked under your feet. Allison was too young to grasp the idea of Christmas, but Betsy had just turned four and was counting the days. "The snow will make Santa's trip from the North Pole so much easier!" she exclaimed, dancing around the room, unable to control her excitement.

The excitement was not for the children alone. We had moved into an old Victorian in the center of town only weeks before, a house that personified Christmas with a red carpet running through the first floor hall and up the stairs, just waiting for dignitaries like Santa to "take the walk." The big front room was still unfurnished, leaving lots of space for our enormous tree, its lights casting a palette of color on the snow-speckled front lawn. And most importantly, Frank and I were steeped in joy, anticipating the birth of our new baby.

Before I became pregnant this time, I'd had a recurrence of ulcerative colitis, a debilitating intestinal disorder, and had been taking a prescribed medication. As I approached the end of my first trimester, my obstetrician suggested that I see a specialist in gastroenterology regarding the effect the disease and medication might have on my pregnancy. With no such specialty care offered in Greenfield at the time, he referred me to a doctor in Boston.

"Don't worry, Mary," my obstetrician assured me. "This is just a routine precaution."

But I was frantic, counting the days until we met with the specialist, terrified of what he might tell us.

I shared my anxiety with my mother, who reminded me that I'd been equally anxious about my other pregnancies, even though my health was fine. She thought I worried excessively. I couldn't contextualize my concern. I just felt trapped in it.

Frank and I drove to Boston on a beautiful June day, leaving the girls with our neighbor Gretchen for the afternoon. My parents lived close by, so my mother planned to walk to our house to fix dinner and stay with the girls until we returned. She was mad about her granddaughters. A day didn't go by that she didn't see her babies. They'd play outside, enjoy the extra attention and snuggle with their "Mimi." Frank was calm, focused on the drive, but I sat in the car wrapped in a bubble of fear.

We arrived on time for our appointment, and the doctor saw me with almost no wait. The exam was routine: a couple of pushes to my belly along with the regular vital sign checks and then lots of questions about the history of my colitis and current lack of symptoms.

"I feel certain that your health is fine," he said, "and the drug you were taking should have no effect on your pregnancy. Other patients have taken the same medication with no problems."

Relief covered me like a warm bath.

We celebrated with an early dinner at Jimmy's Harbor Side, one of our favorite restaurants on the Boston waterfront. For the first time in a long while we talked about our coming baby without all the worry. The smells and sights of a beautiful June evening embraced me, leaving me with a sense of peace and good fortune almost too good to be true. I couldn't wait to tell my mother the wonderful news, even though I felt an "I told you so" coming.

Fireflies blinked across the back lawn as Frank and I walked hand in hand to the door just after dusk. While he fumbled for keys, the door suddenly burst open. Light flooded the night as Gretchen reached past me and pulled Frank into the kitchen. I stood in a daze, feeling a flutter of anxiety, but my emotions had shifted so much in one day, I couldn't hold onto it. Where was my mother?

Frank grabbed me and put his arms around me. "Your mother's dead," he blurted.

I pulled back and looked up at him. "What do you mean, my mother's dead?"

Frank was talking but his words were lost in a deafening echo – *your mother's dead, your mother's dead, your mother's dead . . .*

"Where's my mother?" I demanded. I needed to tell her the good news.

Gretchen began to explain.

My mother had collapsed while walking to our house. A neighbor at the end of the street rushed out to the sidewalk, helped her into her house and called an ambulance. My mother died of an aortic aneurism during emergency surgery. She was 65 years old.

Robot-like, I bought a dress, went to the funeral, thanked friends and family for their sympathy. The sun hung steadfastly in the sky. People gardened and shopped. I wanted to shout, "Stop. Don't you understand? My mother is dead!"

I had felt so lucky to have my parents nearby. But who would pamper and spoil my children now? Who would assure me I was doing a good job as a mother, provide an extra pair of hands, and offer unconditional love to my family? Her death ripped an irreplaceable thread from the fabric of my life.

Shortly after my mother died my father shared a stunning family secret with me. My mother had been adopted as an infant in 1905, and because of the stigma associated with adoption at the time, the secret was ferociously protected. After she and my dad were married, they tried unsuccessfully for years to have a child before adopting my brother, Dave, in 1937. Two and a half years later my mother became pregnant. I was born on June 18, 1940, my father's 42nd birthday.

My mother loved her whole family deeply, but my daughters and I were her legacy from a legacy lost, a reconnected bloodline – her own.

Grief is a strange thing. It lurks just below the surface, bubbling quietly, and can erupt at any moment. Like a powerful wave, it drowned the relief I had brought back from Boston. Its sharp edges cut into my soul and left me with a sense of anxiety about the future.

As summer turned to autumn and my belly grew big, my emotions were at war. Coming home from an obstetric appointment full of excitement about our baby, suddenly I'd find myself in tears as grief struggled to take the upper hand.

Slowly, joy began to win. I even found myself dancing around the kitchen singing, "Yummy, yummy, yummy, I've got love in my tummy," to my little girls' great delight.

The combination of the move, a new baby and Christmas might easily have brought me to my knees, but it had just the opposite effect. More organized and energized than for any Christmas before or since, I had everything in place by the first week in December.

I made dozens of Christmas cookies with the girls, and our tree was in a pail of water on the back porch. My shopping was done, and my Christmas cards were signed and addressed, waiting for one last detail: the announcement of our new baby.

In 1969 we had no way to know the gender of our babies ahead of time. Rather than a pink or blue theme, my cards featured a picture of Betsy and Allison dressed in holiday red and white, with space for me to write in the news of our newborn.

Our heads were bursting with the possibility of real magic. Sometimes before going to sleep, Frank and I lay in bed reminiscing about Christmas mornings when we were kids. Frank had two brothers and a set of twin sisters. Maybe because the girls were often treated like two halves of the same person, Frank's family was a boy family, and boys' toys carried the day. "We always had an electric train going around the tree," he remembered. "And on Christmas morning we woke up to basketball hoops, toy trucks, skis and skates."

He'd never complained about assembling a toy stove or a Barbie dollhouse, but the more we talked, the more he voiced his desire for a son – how much fun it would be to assemble a hockey game or set up an army of toy soldiers. "I want to build something I can play with, too."

That Christmas was indeed filled with dreams.

My labor began early on December 19th. The hospital where my mother had died six months earlier was less than a mile from our house, so the snowstorm that had begun the night before wasn't a problem. After an easy labor, our son was born, Franklin Farnsworth Fitz, Jr. "Jay" had a beautiful round head covered with light brown fuzz, small flat ears, a little nose and a long body with all his fingers and toes, a beautiful, healthy baby to complete our winter wonderland.

We left the hospital on Christmas Eve, five days after Jay's birth, coming home to a house full of the sights and smells of Christmas. My in-laws, my brother and sister-in-law, my dad and a handful of neighbors and friends had gathered to celebrate the holiday and to share in our blessing.

When our guests had left and we had hung our stockings, I took out the antique Christmas ornament that had been my mother's as a child. A white glass bell, small and fragile, it was kept packed in a box of cotton separate from the other ornaments, and we always put it on the tree just before we went to bed on Christmas Eve. Sadness welled up in me as Frank lifted Betsy up to the highest branches, to attach her Mimi's bell to a place of honor.

Suddenly I could feel my mother's presence. She had been with me all along: when we drove home from Boston with our good news, when I first held Jay in the hospital, and now at this moment.

Before going to bed that Christmas Eve, I looked in on our children, kissing each of our sleeping daughters, and then our perfect son.

LESSON 3

*Our hearts expand to accommodate intense
love for another child. Hold onto
this love. It will sustain you in the future.*

Chapter 4

Cautious Hope

Thunk, thunk, thunk. Jay had awakened from his nap, but rather than cry out to be picked up, he rocked violently. Downstairs in the kitchen I could hear the crib scraping along the floor and the sickening thunk, thunk, thunk of his head banging against the headboard.

At almost two years old, Jay displayed an array of full-blown autistic behaviors. He understood few words and made no effort to talk. With his tolerance for frustration at near zero, the calm disposition he had as an infant gave way to kicking, screaming and biting tantrums that erupted more and more frequently. Anything he could reach he'd throw, and if he couldn't grab anything, he struck out with his fists. He pushed his teeth into the heel of his thumb, sometimes until it bled.

I didn't know what set Jay off. I couldn't comfort him. Was he hurting? Did he want or need something? Tantrums became his language, and I had to translate. I tried holding him tightly in my arms. Nothing worked.

I wanted my mother to come for a cup of tea, to talk, to laugh, and even to cry. Her wisdom would have provided balance, and balance was hard to come by.

Frank started to respond more forcefully to Jay's fits of temper and aggression. "Damn it, Mary, we trained our dog. We should be able to train our child!"

He shouted at Jay, spanked his diapered bottom and put him in his room. I shuddered but was glad he intervened where I felt I was failing. Some days were relatively peaceful. Some were sheer hell.

In the midst of one of Jay's tantrums, Betsy took a jar of jelly out of the refrigerator. Slippery with condensation, it dropped on the floor and smashed to pieces.

"Betsy," I screamed, "Look what you've done. How could you be so careless?"

Bursting into tears, she retreated to the family room, choking on her sobs. "I'm sorry, Mommy. I didn't mean to drop it."

Leaving the mess on the floor, I flew up the stairs with Jay, put him in his crib and returned to comfort her. "I wasn't angry with you, sweetheart."

That night we snuggled in her bed and read a story. When she drifted off to sleep, I held her in my arms, feeling an overwhelming need to protect both her and Allison from the pot of emotions boiling over in our house. With my nerves frayed, hanging by a gossamer thread, I was adrift, losing the internal compass that guided my maternal instincts.

Frank and I often went out for a bite to eat on Friday night. Away from the house, we could talk more easily, and our conversation turned to Jay. "God, I'm scared. What's going to happen to him?" I asked. "I worry about his future, but I worry even more about tomorrow and the next day. Some days I'm lost in my guilt."

"Mary, we have two healthy daughters, and you're treating him exactly as you treat them. Stop beating yourself up."

"We just can't do this alone," I answered. "We've got to find someone to help us."

Jay's physician had cautioned, "Don't go to the ends of the earth looking for miracles." But I couldn't relinquish the search and kept reading whatever I could find, searching for some kernel of hope.

I began attending conferences sponsored by the newly formed Massachusetts Association for Mentally Ill Children and the National Society for Autistic Children. At my first conference in Boston, I stepped out of isolation. Other parents were entrenched in the same battle I was fighting. Some mothers told me I was lucky.

"Your son sleeps through the night. My six-year-old screams day and night, sleeping only a few hours at a time."

"We padlock our refrigerator. Otherwise our ten-year-old boy would dump everything out on the floor."

One couple had almost no furniture in their house because their autistic child destroyed whatever was in the room.

While we shared some level of empathy, each of us was locked in our own version of hell.

The conferences featured speakers from new schools and programs designed to address the critical needs of parents desperately looking for help for their autistic children, but none was anywhere near Greenfield. At that time public schools were under no obligation to provide any services at all. The term "early intervention" had yet to be coined. The conferences were important, but I was needed more than ever at home, orchestrator of peace and order, provider of love and safety, all the time wondering if I had the emotional strength to do it all.

Then an idea began to percolate.

Several years earlier I had been asked to help organize and teach the first federally funded Head Start program in our town. Some of the kids we served had a variety of behavioral problems and were referred to the Franklin County Mental Health Center, housed in a brown shingled former private residence right in the heart of Greenfield.

Frank had no recollection of the Mental Health Center. I didn't remember a lot about it either, but I wondered if its professionals might provide services, or at least serve as a resource, for Jay.

"I think it's worth a shot. What do you think?"

"I'm behind whatever you decide, Mary. You know more about this than I do."

Making that phone call was gut-wrenching. The stigma associated with mental health issues was pervasive and facing Jay's autism as a mental disorder killed me. I feared I'd be judged and blamed, and was terrified to open another door only to find no help for Jay on the other side. But I had nowhere else to turn.

With Frank's encouragement, I met with the social worker at the Mental Health Center.

Harriet was an older woman who seemed to hyperventilate as she "oohed" and "aahed" and "oh deared" through the intake process.

"He makes no eye contact," I said.

"Oh dear," she replied.

"He sits and rocks endlessly."

"Oh my," she answered.

Harriet's responses intensified my fears.

I was referred to Dr. K, a young psychologist with a newly minted PhD. Frank, Jay and I were scheduled to meet with him in December, just before Jay's second birthday.

Dr. K appeared genuinely interested. "I feel specific approaches and therapies will assist you with Jay, but first I'd like to do some cognitive tests."

For the first time, someone offered specific tools and services. Full of cautious hope, I returned with Jay in January for testing.

Dr. K brought us into the playroom and sat at a low table with Jay while I sat in a chair against the wall behind him. As long as the directions were nonverbal, Jay performed quite well, putting shapes into appropriate places and lifting one object to find another. In this nonverbal arena, he tested at 23 months. Not bad for a 24-month-old.

But as soon as Dr. K moved on to verbal commands, Jay was lost.

"Put the lid on the box." No response.

"Touch the doll's nose, Jay." He appeared not to hear.

"Point to the doll's bellybutton." Nothing.

Then Dr. K said, "Touch the doll's eyes." Jay immediately put his finger on one of the doll's eyes.

I wasn't entirely surprised. Since infancy Jay had been fixated on eyes. He poked and pushed on his lids. Whenever he could reach the eyes of others, including our dog, he poked at them as well. So here was a word – eyes – that he understood. Here was proof he could learn. And Dr. K had a plan.

He'd recently begun working with two other young

children. Although each of these kids had different developmental and emotional difficulties, he believed the families shared common concerns. "What would you think of forming a parental support group?" Dr. K asked.

What did this mean? Did he think he could help Jay? Eager to find out, I counted the days until our first meeting, scheduled for the following week.

LESSON 4

Leave no stone unturned. Seize every opportunity. Pick up the phone.

Chapter 5

A New Tool

We sat nervously in a circle on folding metal chairs, Frank and I, two other couples and Dr. K. The room had no other furniture. White paint covered the faint remnants of flowery wallpaper in what was once an upstairs bedroom. There we waited to talk publicly about the most painful aspect of our lives. It was one o'clock on a wintry Monday afternoon in January 1972.

Jay was the youngest of the children in our group. One couple's four-year-old son was delayed physically and socially, and the other's five-year-old daughter was schizophrenic. Dr. K encouraged us to talk about the challenges we faced. With my fear of being judged always lurking just below the surface, I described our family's daily life with Jay. As our stories unfolded, warmth filled the stark room. From different walks of life and with different sets of problems, we were bound by a deep love for our children and an intense desire to help them.

Dr. K told us about a technique he thought might be useful. "Each of you has spoken of the general difficulties in your day-to-day lives," he said. "Now I want each of you to focus on a specific problem, just one behavior that's particularly difficult. Give it a minute, but come up with just one thing."

"That's a tall order," I said. "There are so many."

Frank and I agreed that Jay's hitting was our biggest problem. It affected everyone in the family, and I wasn't convinced it was always the result of anger. I was more inclined to see it as an attempt to communicate. He often hit one of his sisters when they entered a room where he was "playing," as if saying, "Here I am. Pay attention to me." They were too young to understand, and over and over I needed to comfort one of them after a random strike.

Each of the other two couples also came up with one troublesome behavior.

"Now we're going to look at ways to help," said Dr. K, "by altering one behavior at a time."

There it was: our introduction to behavior modification, a forerunner to applied behavior analysis. None of us had ever heard of it. It seems unimaginable today, but in 1972 the technique was a relatively new weapon in the war chest of mainstream psychology.

"Stripped to its simplest form," Dr. K continued, "it means you reward your child for appropriate behaviors and chastise him for negative ones."

I wondered how anything so simple could really make a difference, but I was more than willing to give it a try. The others in the group were on board as well, and we all agreed to a weekly meeting. Dr. K showed us how to chart the frequency of our kids' problem behaviors during the coming week.

Behavior therapy has had its share of both proponents and critics over the years. Some professionals still prefer psychoanalysis. Many times while I waited at the Mental Health Center, a father came in with a teenage boy who had no speech. He only clucked like a chicken. Each week he met with a psychiatrist, but in all my time at the Center, I never saw progress. The boy just clucked.

Dr. K's enthusiasm for the behavioral method was contagious. At our second meeting we discussed appropriate responses to the targeted behaviors. We were to respond to Jay's hitting by removing him to his room with a firm reprimand, "No hitting!" Dr. K emphasized the need to use the exact same words – always – and to praise him when he was gentle. We charted each incident. There it was in black and white. Hitting incidences dropped measurably during that first week.

After working for several weeks on Jay's hitting, I decided to apply this behavioral approach to his eating. He still couldn't drink from a cup. He couldn't seem to get his bottom lip in the right spot. Worried that he wasn't getting enough liquid, I had been giving him milk and juice in a bottle. And since he rejected all but a few solid foods, I supplemented his diet with the junior foods he liked.

During that winter of 1972, Jay got a stomach bug and stopped eating altogether except for his bottle and a few bites of applesauce or oatmeal. He lost a little weight and his healthy color. I discussed the issue with our group.

"Try offering Jay a spoonful of junior food that he likes," Dr. K suggested. "When he pushes it away or spits it out, spank his hand and remove him from the table. It may take a few tries, but I bet it'll work."

Sure enough, after a couple of interventions, Jay accepted the whole jar of food. He continued to eat other junior foods, gained weight and his rosy color returned.

In today's world the idea of a spank, even to a diapered bottom or a hand, is anathema to many. While the culture of discipline in the early 70s was different, I worried about spanking. I also worried about other choices we made to help Jay deal with his world.

We were making progress, and I felt I was gaining some control, but I agonized over so many decisions. I had to stand firm for my own sanity and for the sake of my son. I was traveling unmapped territory.

I recently read that singer/songwriter Jonathan Coulton said when he was with his young son, "on playgrounds I mostly spend my time having imaginary arguments with other parents who are secretly judging me."

As the mother of a child with autism, my fear was magnified ten-fold. When friends offered advice, I assumed they had the best of intentions, but often wondered what they said in my absence.

Comments like, "If he were our child, my wife would stop at nothing to find help," or "If you just ignore the tantrums they'll go away," cut to my core. Most of my friends just didn't get it. Jay was different. Ignoring his behavior would not change it, and I *was* searching for resources. Often I left conversations feeling burned.

The weekly meetings with the other parents at the Mental Health Center provided the support I desperately craved. When I expressed frustration and discouragement, they understood.

At conferences, educators, therapists and physicians from across the country described their programs and their theories. I distilled a profusion of information into what I believed would be useful – special diet? medication? and, yes, behavior therapy.

Behavior therapy was emerging as an effective method, used at many special programs from Massachusetts to

California. Though without access to those programs, I felt energized and reassured, convinced we were on the right track.

I couldn't wait to tell the pediatric neurologist in Boston about our newfound tool. Naively ready to "explain" details of our work with Jay, I looked forward to a February appointment. We hadn't seen Dr. D since the previous June, long before my contact with the Mental Health Center.

"I'm not convinced of the effectiveness of the behavioral approach," he said. "It can simply create mechanical responses, but it probably can do no harm."

I was crestfallen. We didn't intend to turn Jay into an automaton, a Pavlov's dog. We intended to help him learn to control his own behaviors. But while Dr. D was critical of our approach, he again offered no alternative. This time I felt angry, not beaten. I was determined to stick with what felt right.

While the realization would not hit me immediately, I was embarking on a soul-searching process that would become the foundation of Jay's treatment for many years to come. As I explored the options, I came to realize that the decisions about his treatment were solely mine. Frank consistently backed me up, but I had to take the initiative. And I couldn't depend upon doctors or friends. I needed to come to grips with the choices. Did I have it in me?

Jay's autism pierced my heart from the first moment I came face-to-face with it. But rather than hide or deny it, I needed to fight with all the force I could muster.

A long crusade lay ahead. I was ready to follow myself into battle.

LESSON 5

Stick with what works.
Keep the effective therapy going.

Chapter 6

Warrior

Dr. K suggested creating an eight-week summer preschool program for a handful of children who were being seen at the Center. Parents would participate as teachers/therapists under Dr. K's supervision along with his wife, Carol, who had no formal training but was as passionate as the rest of us. We found a church basement for our little "school." I hired a babysitter for my girls and spent every morning working with Jay. We were creating our own "early intervention" program.

I was filled with optimism, but the first day was a disaster. At two and a half, Jay was the youngest child in the group and the only one with autism. While the four and five-year-olds had developmental delays and other emotional issues, they knew how to interact and to play.

When Carol lined up the kids to "pretend" to be a train, Jay was lost. They dragged him along anyway, terrified, confused and crying. The warrior in me kicked in. "You're expecting four-year-old behavior from a two-year-old boy with autism," I said to Dr. K. "Jay has no idea how to pretend."

Pretend, or "representative play," is central in the lives of children. A toy car cruising along the floor in your hand represents a real car. But to Jay a toy car was merely the sum of plastic or metal parts. He lined up his matchbox cars, then lay on the floor and stared at them, never making one move. Or else he broke them into pieces.

Dr. K and I talked it out. We agreed to focus on individual therapy for Jay except when a group activity was appropriate. And we established some goals. The first was to continue to address Jay's eating problems. "I'd like to remove all bottles and junior foods," Dr. K said, "and wait for him to be hungry enough to eat table foods."

This approach had seemed too Draconian before. It went against my instincts. My role was to nurture, not to deprive. "There is no way I can do this," I said.

Dr. K convinced me to give it a try. The next day I brought Jay to school for breakfast. He was offered juice from a cup, pieces of toast and banana. He cried, rejecting the food at first, but hunger won out. In two days he mastered a cup completely, and a little at a time he learned to accept an assortment of solid foods.

Reinforced by these victories, we focused our work with Jay on following directions. He had almost no word understanding, so we began with simple commands.

"Come get your juice." If he reached out, we gave him a sip of juice.

"Bring the ball to Mommy." A treat would be waiting for him.

He began to respond to a few simple commands.

That summer we made our trips to the Cape without bottles or baby food jars. I was so proud of Jay. He started to fill out, became as brown as a berry, and his hair bleached out to a soft sandy blond. A snapshot would show a handsome two-and-a-half year old in little plaid overall shorts and no shirt, a beautiful, typical little boy, but a moving picture would show something quite different. We still had a long way to go.

L E S S O N 6

Set realistic goals. Tackle one at a time.

Chapter 7

Covering Our Bases

A light drizzle fell on our windshield as we approached the imposing entrance of Massachusetts General Hospital in Boston on a gray November day. At Dr. D's recommendation, we planned to leave our baby here in the hands of strangers for all kinds of tests. The building's vertical lines beckoned toward the sky in cold arrogance, ignoring us as we entered. The chill went straight to my heart.

Just shy of Jay's third birthday, we'd taken him for another appointment with Dr. D. I couldn't wait to tell him about our progress, even though he didn't think much of the behavior modification method. After chatting with us briefly, he turned to Jay, trying to engage him with words. Jay had no response.

"Jay's cognitive development isn't what I had hoped to see at this point," he said. "His self-stimulatory behaviors (stimming), hand flapping and rocking are more pronounced."

Deflated, I knew in my heart he was right. While we'd made strides toward a better life for Jay, he was stuck developmentally.

"I'd like to have Jay come to Mass General as an inpatient to be evaluated by a team of specialists. Our psychologists, speech pathologists and neurologists will be able to offer insights. And we'll have an opportunity to rule out potential physical issues."

The idea of leaving Jay with people who didn't know him unnerved me. Without speech, he had no way to communicate his needs. But I was desperate to learn, hopeful at the prospect of a detailed evaluation. On the way to Boston with Jay two weeks later, I felt sick to my stomach. While ready for the battle to help my son, I abhorred the process. I feared something terrible might be uncovered. I was anxious about my decisions and as paranoid as ever of being judged by people who didn't know me.

Inside the hospital, a warm pediatric staff took us directly to a cheerful playroom filled with toys and books. There we met another couple who had just arrived from Indiana with their two-year-old autistic son, Lance.

Having never met a child with autism other than Jay, I was astounded and fascinated by the similarities between them. Both engaged in repetitive rocking and hand-flapping. They ignored each other as well as everyone else in the room. Neither made any eye contact nor had any speech. Both made odd noises – Jay's EEEEEEE, Lance's repetitive clicking. Jay stared at the toys and books, rubbed them and even licked them, but like Lance, he had no idea how to play with them.

While I was chatting with Lance's mother, his father suddenly cruised into the conversation. "My reading tells me that autistic children have parents with superior intelligence."

He was probably trying to validate us as parents, but his words seemed to come straight from Dr. Leo Kanner's studies, sans the "refrigerator mother." Sensitive to Lance's dad's thoughts but uncomfortable with his conclusions, I took my "very smart and frosty" self away from the conversation. Logic told me that believing in one part of Dr. Kanner's parent assessment necessitated adhering to the other.

After a short wait in the playroom, a nurse took us to a bedroom with two cribs where Lance and Jay would sleep. I had made arrangements to stay in Boston with an old college friend but would be able to stay with Jay from the time he awoke until I put him to bed. Still, leaving him that first night tore me apart.

"Don't worry," a nurse assured me. "You can stay with him until he falls asleep."

The next morning I learned that Jay had slept through the night, just as he did at home. That news helped me sleep as well.

Jay underwent a battery of tests – an electroencephalogram, blood work and cognitive evaluations by psychologists and speech specialists. I was able to stay with him for all but the encephalogram. He showed no fear of any of the doctors or technicians, but he cried when they drew blood. The toughest part for me was to hold him still. Knowing Jay had no verbal understanding, I could only hold him tightly and sing, little comfort in the face of a stranger wielding a needle.

During the day between tests, we hung out in the playroom with other families. At mealtimes the hospital provided Jay's favorite foods.

After four long days, Frank came to take us home. We tried to keep our conversation light and upbeat, focusing on the positive information the tests might provide, rather than the frightening possibilities of the unknown.

"You know what?" Frank quipped. "Jay just had his head examined."

I laughed, but when we stopped at a Howard Johnsons, Jay became agitated, humming noisily and making incoherent sounds. We tried to hurry through lunch, but before we could finish, the hostess asked us to leave. Embarrassed and hurt, we hustled out, conscious of other patrons' stares. I wanted to scream, "Somebody help us, understand us, be kind!"

But there was no one to listen. We rode home in silence.

During our follow-up at Mass General, we learned that all of Jay's tests had come back negative. While ruling out physical problems was a huge relief, it didn't change Jay's diagnosis, nor did it put us any closer to finding therapeutic services. But Dr. D said something that day that seared my brain like a branding iron. "If Jay develops functional speech by five, he has a good chance of catching up to his peers."

Speech – how elusive. Yet I clung to those words.

Despite everything, I believed if I could reach him I could teach him to speak, to listen, to become a part of us. But without speech, or some way to communicate, Jay remained isolated.

LESSON 7

Eliminate all suspicions and concerns.
Then focus on what you know.

Chapter 8

Family and Friends

During the summer before Jay turned two, the symptoms of my ulcerative colitis, later diagnosed as Crohn's disease, had returned: a constant low-grade fever, virulent diarrhea, loss of appetite and weight. The medicine seemed to become less and less effective, the disease more and more powerful. The exhaustion was debilitating, turning the smallest chores into monumental challenges.

I needed to nap every day just to make it through. That summer a family visited us on the Cape, good friends who were sympathetic but didn't get it. The dad made what he thought was an amusing observation. "If you don't stop spending so much time in bed, you're going to get bed sores."

His comment was met with a great round of laughter. I laughed, too, but the humor was lost on me.

My mother-in-law didn't understand my need to rest either. I was very fond of her and we got along well, but while she was an attractive woman full of fun and energy, she wasn't a nurturer. She'd make comments like, "Why are you taking a nap on this beautiful day?"

The children couldn't possibly understand why I needed to be in bed so much of the time. How could they understand when so many adults didn't?

By fall my condition became critical. I developed a rectal fistula, a rupture in the wall of my lower intestine. It required surgery, a hospital stay and a painful recovery.

I asked my mother-in-law to stay with the children at my house where she would have the support of my babysitters and friends, but she insisted on having them come to her house in Connecticut. It was the only time my in-laws looked after the children, a Herculean task, and it was a disaster. How I longed for my mother.

When I returned home after my surgery and the children were back from Connecticut, my friends got organized. For more than a week, dinner arrived every evening, and one of my friends took Jay for a good part of each day until I gained strength. Frank stayed close to home during that time and helped in the evenings.

My dad, the children's "Ampa," had remarried, to a widow who had been my mother's matron of honor. Both my brother and I were happy he found such a wonderful partner. Dad sold the house in Greenfield, bought a home outside of town, and their gardens became a great source of fresh vegetables, fruit and flowers. Their small, cozy house sat on six wooded acres on a hilltop in the midst of an apple orchard. I loved to bring the children there to walk along the path leading to a beaver dam or to pick apples in the fall.

But my dad and his new wife had a hard time dealing with Jay. They really didn't like having him in the house, and my fastidious father sometimes followed Jay around with the vacuum cleaner. When I get a little compulsive picking up after my own grandchildren, my girls say, "Look out! Mom's pulling an Ampa."

My dad was never unkind to Jay; he simply didn't know what to make of him. One day he said, "Mary, why don't you look for a place for Jay to live, a place where he can be taken care of apart from the family. The burden is killing you."

"Dad," I replied, "I love Jay. He's not a burden. He's my son, and I know with time and the proper resources, I can help him to grow and flourish."

Frank's father was even more difficult. He simply couldn't put up with Jay. Our visits to the Cape often left me in tears when Grandpa Fitz lit into Jay for . . . well, just being Jay. Sometimes his impatience became absurd.

When Jay was not yet three, we joined our extended family to celebrate Thanksgiving on the Cape. I put an appetizer on the coffee table in the living room, and Jay mushed his hand right into the middle of the dish. Instantly his grandfather attacked him verbally. Jay didn't remotely understand the words, but he got the tone. He responded the only way he knew how. He bit his grandfather in the leg.

Jay's mouth couldn't provide words, but it could convey his feelings. The bite set off another explosion of angry expletives, but everyone else in the room silently cheered for Jay, the underdog.

Jay's grandparents were generous with invitations to visit, and while they tolerated him, they weren't able to embrace him and love him for who he was. Sometimes I expected too much of those closest to me, setting myself up for disappointment.

A few close friends became my saviors. They came to my rescue during the more frequent acute Crohn's attacks. They volunteered to take Jay for an afternoon, invited one of the girls for a day, or offered to help with chores requiring two people. Jay was terrified of having his hair cut, so going to the barber was out of the question. I tackled the job at home but couldn't do it alone, so a good friend held Jay while I cut – or was it the other way around? It didn't matter. These small acts of help and understanding were treasured gifts.

But most people I met during the course of a day had no understanding at all. More than once when I explained to someone that Jay was autistic, the reply was, "Oh, he's artistic, how nice."

One of my friends had a son, Scott, who was six months older than Jay. We often got the boys together for one-on-one play, and Scott interacted wonderfully with Jay. If Jay ran up and down my front hall, Scott gleefully followed. Jay didn't know how to imitate Scott or to pretend with him, but he loved to have Scott chase him.

Many of my friends had preschoolers and once or twice a week we got together, giving the kids a chance to play and the moms time for adult conversation. But some friends began to exclude me as Jay got bigger and his behaviors more difficult to control. While we had reduced his hitting, he had little self-control, throwing toys and running around wildly.

Once he put his hand in the coffee creamer and upended the sugar bowl – not exactly socially acceptable behavior. Hurt by the subsequent rebuffs, I also knew that these gatherings were less and less productive for Jay, that the one-on-one visits were best. Invitations dwindled. I felt isolated.

Soon after my return to Greenfield as a young bride, I had become friendly with a woman who also had recently married. As couples we had a great time together, and she and her husband became "aunt" and "uncle" to my children.

She liked to call about five o'clock, a tough time of day with three small kids, but if I had help from Sesame Street, the call was a welcome distraction. When I answered the phone I heard the tinkling of ice in her glass before I heard her voice and as time wore on, her scotch became an increasingly debilitating habit. A nursery school teacher, my friend liked to think of herself as an expert in child development, and as Jay approached preschool age, she offered endless advice.

Many of her ideas were sound: simple suggestions for preschool birthday parties, appropriate gifts for four-year-olds, and encouraging the development of pre-reading skills in young children. But as time wore on and she sank deeper into alcohol, I found much of her advice irrational. It was difficult to pull away from such a sincere and generous friendship, but it was becoming destructive. I decided to step back and keep my own counsel, a good decision, but one that increased my isolation.

Frank and I liked to go out with friends for an occasional movie, and one evening we saw *One Flew Over the Cuckoo's Nest*. As we left the theater, everyone was laughing and talking about Jack Nicholson's funny performance, about the absurd scenes in the asylum.

But I was blindsided. The movie terrified me. Would people want to put Jay in a place like that one day? Could he become a sick, vulnerable inmate? This wasn't rational thinking, simply an irrational fear of the unknown.

I didn't laugh. Instead the movie triggered an explosion of grief. I grieved for myself and for my son, for my inability to function normally with friends, for having to be constantly on guard, making excuses to strangers, and for knowing I would never know the joy of raising a typical boy.

LESSON 8

Spend time with people who are a positive influence on you and your child. They provide amazing strength.

Chapter 9

Speech

If Jay develops functional speech by five, he has a good chance of catching up to his peers. Speech, the very essence of our humanness.

Focused on this important goal and with guidance from Dr. K, I began a daily routine. Every morning before breakfast, Jay and I sat opposite each other at our kitchen counter. I opened a container of his favorite yogurt – Dannon's Boysenberry.

"Jay, look at me," I said.

With each glance, however small, I gave him a mouthful of yogurt.

"Good looking at me!" I used the same words each time. Charting his responses, I began to see progress.

"Yay!" his sisters shouted when I praised Jay for making eye contact. The cheering section may not have meant much to Jay, but it got Betsy and Allison involved. Betsy sometimes became the therapist, offering her brother bites of yogurt as she encouraged him to look at her, and we all cheered for his success.

From eye contact, we moved on to sounds, using the same approach.

"Ma ma ma," I said, encouraging him to repeat the sound.

He was beginning to get the idea and would sometimes say "mmmmm," earning a bite of yogurt and praise. I tried to get him to repeat the hard "d" sound when he wanted to get "down" from his stool, but this proved too much.

While our weekly meetings with Dr. K and the group provided guidance for home therapy, I knew Jay needed more. Dr. K told me an intern from Hampshire College who would be starting at the Center in the fall was particularly interested in special education and speech development. He thought "Jane" would be a good match for Jay.

Jane began meeting with Jay once a week. Her methodology was the antithesis of behavior modification. Instead she tried to be as unobtrusive as possible in Jay's presence, following his lead with activities.

I was invited to observe one of their early sessions. If Jay went to the window, she followed and talked softly about what they saw outside. I was more than willing to go along with this approach. It seemed a lot like the time I spent with Jay when I could get him to relax at home. I also thought that any type of one-on-one therapy was better than none.

Jane's philosophy about autism was different as well. While I was aware that her work with Jay had not been behaviorally oriented, I was blindsided by the passionate opposition she expressed toward that method during a meeting we had with Dr. K.

"Why do you withhold food from him?" she asked. "Why do you insist on changing his behaviors? Do you rock him and cuddle him?" she added, a question that astounded me. "Do you listen to his sounds and talk to him?"

I let this young woman, barely out of her teens, turn on the "guilt tapes" in my head.

In my earnest naiveté, I believed that all the people working with Jay were my partners. But it seemed Jane was coldly studying me as part of the cause of my son's autism. Worse yet, Dr. K never uttered a word of support, neither of the behavioral method nor of me and my commitment to my son.

At the end of her internship, Jane submitted a six-page case summary to Dr. K which he shared with me. In it she concluded that Jay's progress had been excellent. "Perhaps language will begin to develop."

She also wrote, "I don't think Jay needs to be trained in or out of specific kinds of conduct . . . he will acquire certain modes of conduct and reach new levels of social exchange when he is ready to do so, if he is accepted and treated as a human being."

These words added fuel to the fire. My fury and strength overrode the guilt.

I told Dr. K I was hurt by Jane's observations. "She's young and is missing the experience and information needed to come to her conclusions. I hope you guide her to a better understanding of the underlying problem and caution her about hasty judgments."

He tried to calm me down, but I had a weird feeling. Perhaps he felt the same way . . .

During the winter after Jay turned three, Dr. K and his wife, Carol, submitted proposals requesting funds from the Massachusetts Office for Children and from the town of Greenfield to support an early intervention plan patterned after our eight-week summer program. The initiative called "Project Change" would provide a one-on-one behavioral-based curriculum to a small group of preschool children with hard to manage behaviors.

I immersed myself in the battle to fund the project, lobbying both the Office for Children and the town with letters, phone calls and meetings. I had found my voice and was on the front lines. I knew intimately the value of such a program.

But the state and the town wanted Project Change to focus exclusively on underprivileged children from single parent families on welfare. The client profile narrowed. Since the program would be available only to children with families on welfare, Jay became ineligible. Both proposals were accepted and the funding came through, but not for Jay.

My battle continued for Jay to be included. It got ugly at one point when a town selectman stated publicly that we, the Fitzes, could certainly afford to pay for services for Jay. But no such services were available.

I confronted the selectman at his place of business. "Are you not aware that absolutely nothing else is out there for children like Jay?"

"Yes, but you, not the town, should pay for his services," he replied.

The cost for Project Change was prohibitive. "We'd be happy to be assessed and pay accordingly. This program is crucial to Jay's development."

I was tough and outspoken. I succeeded. With help from Dr. K, we struck an agreement with the town, and Jay was accepted into Project Change. I never knew whether that selectman supported my request.

One day I heard an advertisement on the car radio for the Greater Hartford Open Golf Tournament. Sammy Davis, Jr.

would be a celebrity guest with his $30,000 golf cart. I made an entry in my journal when I got home. June 4, 1973: "I'm overwhelmed with frustration and sadness over the idea that someone has a $30,000 golf cart, and I can't get funding to help my special needs son."

The juxtaposition seemed senseless. Where were our values?

During this stressful time of negotiations regarding Project Change, I continued speech therapy at home. *If Jay develops functional speech by five, he has a good chance of catching up to his peers. Functional speech by five* became my mantra.

And then it happened. He said "Hi." A word – not just a sound but a word! It was during one of our sessions at the kitchen counter: he was exactly 3 years 4 months old. While he said it only with my prompting and sounded mechanical, use it he did. Within a week he learned to wave and say "bye-bye" (ba-ba), another real word! These small miracles gave me enormous hope.

Several weeks later, a monumental leap forward – his first spontaneous word. When it was time to leave a friend's house, I got up and stood by her front door. Jay came with his jacket, raised his arms and said, "up, up." Ironically after months of trying to get him to say "down," he spontaneously and appropriately said "up." I whirled him around praising him, smothering him with unwanted hugs and kisses.

He continued to use the word. He'd say, "up, up" to his father to initiate the roughhousing he had just begun to enjoy. I will be forever convinced Jay learned to speak only because he was *taught*, not as a result of any natural developmental speech patterns.

When Jay started Project Change a few months later, at almost four years old, he had three words: "hi," "bye-bye" and "up." Within two months his vocabulary increased to six self-initiated, functional words and a dozen more he repeated when prompted.

"Juice," he said, taking my hand and leading me to the fridge.

"Car," he repeated, taking me to the door.

With language came an emerging ability to handle his environment. He was beginning to be able to make his needs known, and this had a direct impact on his behavior. His tantrums became less frequent, and his head banging stopped completely. We began to see glimpses of a sweet personality.

Project Change was exceeding my expectations. Within six months Jay had a vocabulary of over 60 words and was starting to put some words together. "Up, Mummy, more milk," he said, and "down" finally made the list as well. These simple words were music to my ears.

If Jay develops functional speech by five, he has a good chance of catching up to his peers.

I clung to these words.

Lesson 9

Fiercely pursue communication skills.
Use whatever works: speech therapy,
word boards, computers, sign language.

Chapter 10

Sisters

"Mommy, Mommy, Jay hurt me!"

I raced downstairs to find four-year-old Allison in the family room sobbing. Jay sat on the floor nearby, looking confused and anxious, clutching a plastic school bus in his right hand. I took the weapon from him and picked him up – not gently. Taking two steps at a time, I dashed up to his bedroom and put him in his crib. "No hitting!" I shouted, using a technique learned from our work at the Mental Health Center.

Returning to the family room, I folded Allison into my arms where she choked on her sobs. Betsy reached in to give her sister a hug and impart some of her six-year-old wisdom. "He didn't mean to hurt you, Allie. He doesn't understand."

How many times had I uttered those words to Jay's sisters? Could they understand that the rules of their reality did not apply to their brother?

While we were making progress, the girls were still victims of Jay's outbursts. I believed that he didn't understand, that he was just trying to deal with a world he couldn't control.

Before I brought Jay out of his room, the girls and I snuggled on the couch. "Let's do something fun together," I suggested, "like an arts and crafts project."

I set up the glue, scissors, markers, felt and paper at the kitchen counter, out of Jay's reach. "Okay, what shall we make?" I asked.

"Let's make Daddy some cards," Betsy replied.

"But it's not his birthday," Allison objected.

"That's alright. We'll make some silly pictures to give him when he gets home."

The girls got started and Jay watched from his highchair. Though I had diffused the crisis for the moment, I remained rattled and frustrated. My frustration transferred to Frank when he got home.

I hated myself for nailing him as soon as he walked in the door, but it was happening more and more. When he headed upstairs to change his clothes that evening I followed, slamming the bedroom door behind us. "You have no idea what it's like here all day with these kids," I ranted. "Jay went after Allison again and really hurt her."

My frustration turned to anger as if it were his fault. He got angry too. "I can't be in two places at once," he growled. "Someone has to support this family."

Turning on my heel, I stormed downstairs. The girls were watching Mr. Rogers' Neighborhood, and Jay was sitting on the floor rocking.

"C'mon," I said in my calmest voice. "Let's give the cards to Daddy.

Frank received the cards with enthusiasm, but the situation sat in my gut for the rest of the evening. Was I exasperated? Angry? Yes, but I was also profoundly concerned for Jay's sisters.

At bedtime that evening, after Frank tucked the girls into bed and Jay settled down easily for me, we discussed the events of the day. With anger gone, we focused on the myriad problems that were becoming more and more a part of everyday life.

Betsy was the caregiver, the "other mother" in our family. Allison was the blithe spirit, a happy-go-lucky preschooler who was smaller and less able to defend herself against Jay's aggression.

Our house sat on a corner facing a busy street, but the lot sloped down to the driveway and into a small backyard bordering a quiet tree-lined street. A tall privet hedge that Frank kept neatly trimmed provided both privacy and protection. In nice weather our activity revolved around the backyard, where we had a swing set and a huge sandbox filled with toys.

One day when I was outside with the children, Jay found a piece of metal pipe at the edge of the yard – a tube – and flung it at Betsy. It cut her hand, not badly enough for stitches, but enough to leave a permanent scar.

Betsy cried but didn't get angry with Jay. She loved and coddled her brother, showing great concern about the things he did to hurt himself. Once when he was biting his own hand – or, more accurately, pushing his front teeth against his skin – Betsy offered her own hand instead.

While Betsy worried, Allison marched to her own drummer. Sometimes she marched right out of the driveway and down the street, led by her doll carriage, her little blond head held high as if her carriage contained a prince. I couldn't turn my back on her for a second.

In later years Allison told me that sometimes my preoccupation with her brother "left her to her own devices." I used to say the doll carriage got her into trouble, leading her away from the house, and her escapes were impeccably timed. The neighbors got to know her well.

I felt deeply guilty about devoting an excessive amount of time to Jay. I couldn't chaperone Betsy's field trips or help out in her classroom. And I'd been reluctant to enroll her in dance class because the logistics seemed overwhelming. Swimming lessons at the Y were challenging enough.

Our weekends were affected as well. My sister-in-law lived with her family outside of Boston, and our families got together often before Jay was born. Barrie and I had gone to college together and later married brothers. Her boys were born at about the same time as Betsy and Allison, so we enjoyed many fun visits with the kids. She became the sister I never had.

As Jay grew, our impromptu visits became less frequent. She and her family were wonderful with Jay, but his behaviors made visits at their house more difficult. The house was small and filled with little treasures, including glass shelves in the dining room windows filled with plants. During one visit, Jay became excited, jumping around and flapping his hands, and accidently dislodged one of the shelves, breaking everything to pieces. Since Barrie's house wasn't "Jay-proofed," it became much easier for Barrie and her family to visit us.

During one visit at our house, Barrie and I were sitting in the family room when she asked, "How can you stand the noise?"

"What noise?" I answered.

"You know, Jay's constant humming and the EEEEEEE sound he makes all the time."

"My gosh, I don't even hear it."

Until Barrie brought the sounds to my attention, I was barely aware of them. I heard only the sounds of our household. Jay's sisters seemed oblivious to the noises filling our waking hours, too. My concern for them deepened.

Somehow I needed to change the balance of our family. Time spent with Jay doing behavioral therapy had become sacrosanct, and it was working. But other things could be refocused. Some time needed to be set aside just for the girls.

"I need to reorganize us," I said to Frank.

"Okay," he agreed. "Where do we go from here?"

"Let's plan activities that work for both Jay and his sisters."

One simple thing that came out of the conversation was Frank's decision to finish fencing in the play yard. We scoured the yard for unsafe items Jay could throw and put all the garden tools in the garage. The fence made it so much easier for me to be in the yard with the kids. I could even work in the vegetable garden without Allison pulling her disappearing act and Jay finding dangerous weapons.

We also encouraged the girls' friends to come to our house. We lived near the elementary school and our house became a regular stop for some of Betsy's friends on their way home from school. They called their moms and asked if they could stay and play. Though Jay didn't interact, he was part of the mix, and the children seemed to accept him without much thought. When Allison started school her friends did the same.

One warm spring afternoon when Jay was about three, I dressed him up in my father's first suit, a little navy blue wool sailor suit that had been tucked away in mothballs for decades. A few friends were playing at the house with the girls. "Let's go outside and take pictures of Jay," I said. And everyone wanted to be in the pictures with Jay in his grandfather's suit.

Jay was still afraid of many things. He screamed in terror when I tried to get him on a tricycle, hating having his feet off the ground. We knew skiing would be a disaster, so we didn't even try.

We found the Cape to be a great place for family activities. It amazed me how easily Jay adapted to the change in his environment, a challenge for most people with autism. We all loved to hike, and the Cape Cod Museum of Natural History had trails through the marshes. Jay raced ahead of us, loving the freedom.

But our favorite part of the Cape was the beach, and we frequently picnicked on an outer bar reachable only by boat. During the summer that Jay was four, he often got up in the morning and went straight to his life jacket. "On boat," he'd say, using some of his new vocabulary.

We all have great memories of Jay bending over and putting his head on the sand, using his head to make trenches, for what we'll never know. But we all laughed and accepted the peculiar joy he experienced doing the beach his way.

Jay became "Jaybird" to his sisters, the nickname I had given him as a baby, which morphed to "Bird" to "Birdie." When Betsy was a teenager she took Jay to visit a Chatham friend whose mother had never met Jay. When he went into the bathroom and flushed the toilet continuously, she became alarmed.

"Who is that?" she asked. "Is he okay?"

"Mom," her daughter replied, "that's 'Jaybird.' He's great."

But others didn't see Jay quite that way. We were at Logan Airport in Boston one foggy evening, waiting for Frank to return from a business trip so we could drive to the Cape together for the weekend. The fog had delayed his flight, so we waited in front of a huge glass window. Jay was about six years old and was gleefully making his EEEEEE sound, flapping his hands as he looked at the reflections in the glass. A couple of older kids began to imitate and make fun of him. I spoke firmly to them, explaining Jay's autism.

Betsy's reaction astonished me. "Mom, don't be mad at them. It's too bad they don't understand how far he's come." She didn't see his behavior as bad, nor did it embarrass her. Instead she took pride in how much it had improved. I was so proud of her.

As the girls grew and matured, they protected Jay with incredible affection and compassion. When it was time to write their essays for college admission, both chose to write about their brother, well written, poignant pieces about unconditional love.

As an adult Betsy's thought a lot about her life with her brother. "So many voices needed to be heard that I thought mine was lost," she recently told me. "I stood in the shadows of chaos during those early years. Then I withdrew. But you and Dad set the tone on how to treat Jay, and we followed."

She now believes a piece of her childhood was lost to being a caregiver at a very early age. She says so without resentment, but with an acknowledgment of loss – loss of my attention and an element of her childhood.

"But I would be a different person if not for my brother," she added. "I learned compassion and tolerance and that perfection is not a requirement for goodness."

Allison remembers being upset by Jay's tantrums, afraid that maybe he was hurt, but his behavior never embarrassed her. "You know, Mom, Jay was just my brother, and I loved him."

An acquaintance who had one son delivered a baby girl when the boy was about four years old. The baby had Down syndrome, and the mother refused even to look at her, deciding to give her up for adoption. In spite of reassurances that the child had no heart problems and the condition was not severe, she remained resolute. She was unwilling to risk the "defective" child's interfering with the growth and development of her son.

I was judgmental, horrified by her decision. Yet at the same time I understood her fear. I remembered my own as Jay became a force in our family structure. But by the time she was making her decision, my children were older. Their characters had begun to develop, and I was able to recognize the many ways their lives were deeply enriched by their very special brother.

Our hopes and aspirations can seem tossed into the wind when life throws a curve. But sometimes a challenge can provide an opportunity, the chance to make a real difference in the life of a unique person entrusted to you. Though finding the strength to meet the challenge is not easy, Jay's sisters rose to the occasion.

LESSON 10

Autism is a family challenge.
Keep the family in the loop.

Chapter 11

One Step Back—
Another Forward

Sometimes in the evening I caught myself looking up at the first star and silently reciting a childhood jingle:

Star light, star bright

First star I see tonight.

I wish I may, wish I might

Have the wish I wish tonight.

I pleaded with a twinkling orb millions of miles away to intervene on Jay's behalf, then quickly turned away. It would be bad luck to look at the star after I had made my wish. On nights like these, when I went to bed, I dreamed of Jay running and playing with friends. He would be OK.

Feeling alone and vulnerable, the palette of my emotions was like a Jackson Pollack painting, colors spattered randomly across the canvas of my life.

One day while grocery shopping, I ran into the mother of an old school friend. We chatted about her daughter, who had four boys, and she asked about my children. "Oh how your mother would have loved them," she said. Without any warning I burst into tears right there in the market. Though I tried to paint a positive picture, my emotions were often too close to the surface.

Another high school friend's mother worked at a department store in town. When I saw her she loved to talk about her daughter who had a disabled son born a couple of years before Jay. A gossipy, charming woman whose Catholic faith seemed to sustain her, she liberally sprinkled her conversation with philosophical clichés and platitudes.

"How's Jay doing?" she asked one day.

"He's doing fine," I assured her, "but his autism is a challenge."

"God gives us only what we can handle," she replied with absolute conviction.

But some days I felt I had been dealt a hand I simply couldn't play.

Unlike my friend's mother, I couldn't find God in the everyday. I found Him fleetingly in sunsets and on frozen mountaintops where I believed in a great creative force. I wanted a fully believable God, but when it came to understanding why Jay was born with autism, I was lost.

When the kids were young, I left Jay with Frank on Sunday mornings and took the girls to the Congregational church where Frank and I had been married and the children had been christened. I slipped into the comfort of familiar hymns and rituals while Betsy and Allison were at Sunday school. Sustained by some sense of temporary peace, I dove into the week ahead.

From the stories told by other parents at conferences, I knew my day-to-day life with Jay might have been considerably worse. He went to bed easily, slept through the night and napped on schedule during the day. But every moment he was awake required unremitting supervision to protect him and ward off disasters.

One of Jay's favorite trouble spots was the bathroom. He liked to flush the toilet over and over just to watch the water swirl down the drain. And he added household items, prompting frequent calls to our plumber to unclog the drain. On one visit as he lifted the toilet from the floor, he said, "You know, Mrs. Fitz, you could do this yourself."

"Hmmm," I thought. "I bet I could," so I got a lesson in plumbing 101. I bought a snake, a metal chain-like device, and became the plumber-in-residence. An outside lock on the door helped but the girls often forgot to use it.

When pens or crayons landed in Jay's hands, he wrote on anything in sight: walls, woodwork, floors, tiles.

Even more alarming were Jay's destructive actions toward himself. Besides biting the heel of his hand until it bled, he pulled out his hair, and he dug at his gums with his fingernails until they began to recede.

During these challenging times my young babysitter, Nancy, earned a place on my hero list. She came with us to the Cape for several weeks each summer and became part of the family. A low-key steady girl with quiet wisdom that belied her years, she was undaunted by Jay's bizarre behaviors, and her ability to deal with him was uncanny.

She and the girls painted an old refrigerator carton and cut out windows, creating "Nancy's Modular Home" for imaginative play. "C'mon, Jay," Nancy cajoled. "Come in the house with us." It amused them for days. Jay climbed in and out, peering through the windows, even though he was clueless about pretending the box was a house.

Still obsessed with cylinders, Jay continued to gather tubes. His giant Tinker Toys were made of large plastic tubes, but Jay didn't build with them. Instead he spread them on a tabletop or floor and flapped his hands in front of them. He did the same thing with PVC plumbing tubes.

Jay's "stimming" – flapping and rocking – filled a lot of his waking hours. He also was fascinated with cigarettes, perfect cylinders. Someone snapped his picture on the beach one summer when he was about three-and-a-half, staring down the cylindrical tube of a Whiffle ball bat with an unlit cigarette in his mouth. Amazing that he never took up the habit!

As part of our behavior modification program, we tried to eliminate cylinders from Jay's play. For a while it worked, but he went back to them as soon as he found an opportunity. Those objects that had fascinated him from his earliest years in some way gave him comfort.

When Jay was about two, I took the three children for a photo session. I had never met the photographer, but had spoken at length with him on the phone. He suggested we bring our dog along for the picture.

So I and my little entourage tumbled out of our Toyota wagon on Main Street. Toby, our springer spaniel, was sweet and well-behaved but freaked out when we got to the studio, jumping around and knocking things over. At the same time Jay had a complete meltdown. The scene was utter bedlam.

Just as I was about to give up, Jay reached out to the photographer, who was holding an empty plastic film cylinder. When he handed the cylinder to Jay, he immediately calmed down, sitting peacefully just long enough for a few quick shots.

Toby never made the cut, and the finished product belied the reality: three beautiful suntanned children smiling sweetly into the camera. The empty film tube remained in the picture in Jay's hand. The photographer couldn't wait to get rid of us.

Jay loved his bath. Surrounded by toys and containers, he splashed around for as long as I let him. He was over two when he realized a cup would empty if turned upside down. The discovery entertained him endlessly.

Jay's fascination with the bathroom did not mean toilet training was easy. It was merely delayed. His training began in earnest in the spring of 1973 when he was three-and-a-half, just tall enough to stand up to pee. He feared having his feet off the floor while sitting on the toilet.   He got the idea fairly quickly. By summer he was dry most of the day, but bowel movements were another story.

One day when a terrible stench filled the house, I discovered that Jay had deposited a BM from his diaper into the humidifier in the front hall. So I started sitting him on the pot for a few seconds every day, holding him and talking to him, and he began to get more comfortable. On October 11th, a banner day, Jay had his first BM on the toilet. By the time he was four he was completely toilet trained.

Victories large and small were treasured. One winter afternoon my friend, Sue, came to visit, bringing her daughter to play with Betsy and Allison, and Jay was peripherally involved.   Later I made an entry in my journal. February 1973: "Sue commented on how much better Jay was, that he didn't try once to hit the girls. She said we were doing great with our behavior modification and that she reveled in the commotion and chaos of our house."

I cherished every breakthrough with Jay, every step forward, eagerly recording them in my journal. I also recorded the fear I felt during my illness and the frustration when Jay's progress stalled. April 15, 1973: "I'm depressed and miserable . . . we have reached another plateau, and the bizarre behaviors overshadow the progress."

May 15, 1973: "Gretchen called and said some of my friends got together with their children this morning. I wasn't invited, and I don't know why she told me. I feel hurt and alone."

I felt claustrophobic, smothered by the veil of responsibility. And the strain at home became palpable. Often feeling both physically and emotionally spent, tears came easily as did anger and resentment.

Frank's work often kept him on the road for a couple of weeks a month, and his sports filled many evenings and weekends. In addition he was completing his MBA studies. He loved his children dearly, and when he was in the house he was an energetic participant in the family. He played with the kids, helped with baths and read endlessly to Betsy and Allison.

But he was seldom home. Aside from business travel, his company sponsored many weekend leisure outings for its executives – command performances for him, weekends alone for me. Evenings and bedtimes were especially tough. The time of day poets refer to as "the bewitching hour" was aptly described as the "gangrene hour" by one of my friends.

I loved my husband and treasured the family bond, yet felt disenfranchised from a significant part of his life. And the choices he made when he was at home left me disillusioned and hurt. Once during an acute phase of my Crohn's, he left on a Saturday morning to play basketball. I begged him not to go. Later that day I landed in the hospital with a 105 degree fever.

"I'm leaving on a jet plane. Don't know when I'll be back again." Peter, Paul and Mary's words touched my heart one early morning just after Frank pulled out of the driveway heading for the airport. But the sadness the radio triggered gave way to resentment as the day progressed.

Flying away seemed like a great escape. I knew most often my husband was traveling for business, yet a crescendo of thoughts filled my head when I'd catch sight of an occasional contrail over my backyard. Was the jet taking its lucky passengers to Europe? To ski the Rockies? To relax on a sunny Florida beach, worry-free? My thoughts would dissipate along with the contrail as I returned to my reality: Allison on her big wheel in the driveway, Betsy doing cartwheels on the lawn – and Jay on the swing going back and forth, back and forth, over and over with empty eyes.

I was willing to try almost anything to remove the monster of my disease from my life. I became determined to quit smoking, to look more carefully at my diet, cut back on fat. Call it good sense or dumb luck, but after a few months my symptoms began to subside. Within a year I was symptom-free and had become a long-distance runner. Years later I learned that smoking exacerbates the symptoms of Crohn's disease.

While the condition never completely disappears, I was one of the lucky ones in remission. How different my world looked, unclouded by pain and exhaustion. I needed to be at my best for my family. Gaining strength, the warrior in me triumphed again.

LESSON 11

"How goes the mother, so goes the family" —
especially true with a special needs child.

Chapter 12

Roller Coaster

In spite of reapplying for grants and lobbying, funding for Project Change was going to run out at the end of its first year in June 1974, leaving Jay without educational services again. It was an overwhelming letdown.

So that spring at Dr. K's suggestion, I took Jay to the Child Guidance Center at UMass for a workup. The psychologist suggested we visit the UMass Clinic Nursery School to observe. Just as a teacher pointed to a quiet little boy with Down syndrome, telling me how much the staff enjoyed including special children in the program, Jay grabbed a toy and flung it across the room narrowly missing teachers and children.

I sat him on my lap for a few minutes and quietly scolded him. As soon as I let him down he darted around randomly, unable to comply with classroom directions.

That situation wasn't going to work. Jay needed a program with intensive focus on self-control, and nothing in that environment would provide it.

Dr. K then directed me to a behavioral psychologist in the Education Department at UMass who had students specializing in behavior therapy. With a one-on-one student aide, Dr. K thought Jay might be able to function in the Clinic Nursery School.

But the psychologist only reinforced my own concern that the program would be a bad placement for Jay, even with a student accompanying him, due to its lack of structure. More disturbing, he suggested that I become Jay's full-time behavior manager, devoting 3 to 4 hours a day to language training, etc.

This guy didn't get my world. Already spending a significant part of every day working with Jay, I also had a second grader and a five-year-old who was at home all but two hours a day of kindergarten. I had created as effective a home learning environment for Jay as possible, but I needed help. The weight was becoming unbearable.

But something exciting was brewing in the developing world of special education, something that would change the face of education for special children in this country forever. Bill 766 had just been adopted in the Massachusetts state legislature. Starting in the fall of 1974, every child in the state, from age three to twenty-one, regardless of disabilities, would be guaranteed an education. Regardless of disabilities, guaranteed an education!

Nowhere in our entire country did children with special needs enjoy any guaranteed education whatsoever. Massachusetts was leading the way. Law 766 would provide the prototype for the Education for Handicapped Children Act 94-142, which would eventually become the law of the land. Just how these services would unfold remained a mystery, but I was fueled with irrepressible optimism as I traveled to conferences and meetings, trying get a handle on how other communities were responding to the law.

At the first New England Conference for Autistic and Emotionally Disturbed Children in Worcester, I learned of a school for autistic children in Lawrence, Massachusetts. Behaviorally-based, it offered a full day of educational and therapeutic programs geared to the development of speech, communication and individual academics. I also learned that almost all of the successful curricula in schools throughout the state used at least some level of behavior therapy.

Just knowing such opportunities were out there tantalized me. But the school in Lawrence was two hours away.

Inspired by the program, and with the 766 law in place, I made an appointment with the newly appointed Director of Special Education in Greenfield to tell him about the school in Lawrence. "This is the type of program we need in Greenfield for children like Jay," I said.

He was quick to react. "The town is up against a financial challenge with this new mandate."

"But it's the law," I insisted.

"We're forming the Franklin County Educational Collaborative, to establish services that all the towns in the county can share," he said.

"A county-wide program might be in place soon?"

"We have yet to identify any other children with needs similar to your son's. It will be a while before anything is up and running."

I was astonished.

He referred me to the woman who had just been hired to direct the new collaborative. Our conversation was stilted. She didn't appear interested in behavior therapy and seemed to lack an understanding of the autistic child. She certainly wouldn't be an easy ally.

So I pressed on. During the 1950's Dr. May, the father of autistic twin boys, founded a residential school in Chatham on the Cape. I was aware of the school because of our family home in Chatham, and decided to visit. While I was not interested in residential placement for Jay, its proximity to family and friends warranted a look.

The director and staff were welcoming, but the school unacceptable. The child to staff ratio was high and the environment Spartan, with few toys and pictures. There were no speech therapists or other specialists. It was a far cry from the excellent May Institute of today.

"If only I could pick up a school and bring it home," I said to Frank after yet another visit to a school out of geographic reach, "or pick up our family and go to a school."

Moving had become a topic of many discussions as I learned of facilities in different parts of the state, and we weighed the pros and cons. Frank was on an excellent career track in Greenfield, and we had developed a strong support system, so ultimately we decided to stay and continue to look for options closer to home.

But I was coming up empty-handed, and found myself constantly talking about my frustration. One friend told me about The Children's Language Institute in Ludlow, a half hour from Greenfield, a day school serving aphasic kids (those with no speech) between the ages of three and nine. Should Jay be accepted, transportation would be provided.

I took Jay for an evaluation, but he wasn't an aphasic child. He was slow to speak because he was autistic. After our visit we were told the school was not equipped to deal with his disruptive behaviors.

Another painful rejection, but not a useless visit. One of the speech therapists spoke highly about a school for autistic and behaviorally challenged children at Kennedy Memorial Hospital for Children in Brighton, just outside of Boston.

"It sounds wonderful," I said, "but it's two hours away."

"Yes, but it's a Monday through Friday residential program with the children returning home each weekend. After meeting Jay and knowing what I know about Kennedy, I think it might be a perfect match."

Could I bear Jay being away from home during the week?

I was meeting one roadblock after another. The County Collaborative was slow to get moving, and all the other schools were either too far away or inappropriate. He would be five in December, with no school program available to him.

So I took the name of her contact and called Kennedy. Frank and I went to see the school and to meet with the pediatric neurologist in charge.

At that time, the curriculum at Kennedy was designed for the diagnosis and treatment of autism and other emotional disorders. The objective was not to keep the children indefinitely, but to prepare them for subsequent placement. After a year Jay would have to move on. We hoped by that time a program would be in place in Greenfield.

Our visit was wonderful. The Kennedy program was based on a behavioral model which included a morning preschool component, followed by an afternoon of therapies to address the specific needs of each child. The outdoor playground had swings and toys, and a brand new building under construction would open in the fall, dedicated exclusively to these children. The neurologist suggested a five day assessment to see if Jay would be an appropriate candidate.

"Whew," I said to Frank when we got in the car to leave. "We're suddenly moving at the speed of light. I hope it's in the right direction."

Following that trajectory, in May 1974, we arrived at Kennedy ready to relinquish our son for five days. A staff person directed us down a long gray corridor, and it was like walking through a black-and-white movie – black floors, gray walls, white ceilings, with rooms off to the side. We passed an alcove where iron lungs were stored, a grim reminder of the days before Jonas Salk gave us the polio vaccine. But as we entered the unit where Jay would stay, a burst of color and light greeted us, and the movie suddenly changed to Technicolor.

By the time we reached the bright, cheerful bedroom Jay would share with four other children, I was emotionally shaken. I was able to pull myself together before a staff person came to take Jay onto a lovely sun porch adjacent to the bedroom to join the other kids for lunch. He looked through the window and said in his typical monotone, "Hi," relaxed and comfortable in his new surroundings.

While we were meeting with the neurologist and then a social worker, Jay had an audiology test and then came back to us for chocolate milk and cake, his favorites. But when we kissed him goodbye and started to leave, he said, "Bye Daddy, Mommy," and tried to follow us.

After more hugs and kisses, I turned away and walked numbly to the car, my mind a swirling cyclone. Would Jay be okay without me? Had I done enough to find a quality placement in our own community? But the opportunities offered at Kennedy were like nothing I had ever seen before. Jay deserved a shot at it.

The short stay at Kennedy proved positive for Jay. By phone each day I was told he had adjusted well. We also were told that Jay fit the profile, that he had the potential to grow and flourish given the opportunity.

A social worker from the newly-formed County Collaborative in Greenfield visited Kennedy, along with a teacher from Project Change. They determined it would be an excellent placement for Jay in the fall, funded through the brand new Massachusetts Law 766.

After Jay's year at Project Change, I believed more than ever that he yearned to be released, to be freed from whatever held him captive. The experts at Kennedy agreed.

I wasn't giving up a lost boy. I was loaning a treasure, and loans are temporary.

Lesson 12

Don't let barriers break you down. Break them down.

Chapter 13

A Painful Choice

The beautiful new building at Kennedy Memorial Hospital for Children was ready for its young occupants in September 1974. Adjacent to the main hospital, it was a wonderful facility, custom-made for children with autism and other developmental disorders. The children no longer needed to navigate the hollow gray halls of the main hospital to reach special therapy sessions. Instead, the building was self-contained and designed exclusively to meet the needs of its unique population.

On September 17, we left Jay there for the first time – on loan. Not quite five years old, he cried when we left. I picked him up and hugged him. "I love you my little Jaybird," I whispered in his ear. "I'll watch over you in my heart."

That was the last time he cried when we left him at Kennedy. While he seemed excited to see us when we came back, he also flapped and hummed when he returned, happily taking the hand of a staff member.

Still the process was difficult. I had to learn to accommodate my feelings while we followed through with our painful decisions. Would those charged with his care treat him with kindness and compassion? Respond thoughtfully to his needs? How could anyone love him as I do?

But I was sure that Kennedy was the best place to nurture Jay's potential. The physical setup was perfect, with small bedrooms, two children to a room instead of the dormitory arrangement in the old building, and a state-of-the-art preschool room, a bright space filled with toys, books and equipment designed to help young minds grow.

The children were organized into three units according to age. Jay was part of the youngest group, twelve youngsters who attended preschool every day together from 9:00 to noon and played in the playroom or outdoor play yard between afternoon therapy sessions.

The common denominator in each day was the behavioral approach to all activities. But most important of all were the people: teachers, therapists, aids and social workers who brought the program to life.

Visits to the school in session became part of our own education, helping us to acquire more skills and tools to use at home, and to feel a part of Jay's everyday life.

Betsy expressed the most concern about her brother. "How will they know how to treat him?" she asked when we were getting ready to take him the first time.

"We'll all have a chance to visit," I replied, "so you can see for yourself how he's doing."

The visits were fun for the girls, and a great way to allay Betsy's anxieties. Allison settled right into the preschool room to play with the toys, while Betsy observed her brother and his schoolmates. After a couple of visits they were satisfied that Jay's school was a good, safe place for him.

He became the darling of the Kennedy program, a handsome little boy with a mostly sweet disposition. Members of the staff told us often how much they enjoyed working with him.

A pediatric neurologist supervised the medical component at Kennedy. Medication had been an ongoing discussion with Jay's physicians at home, and the dialogue continued at Kennedy. Dr. D at Mass General had prescribed a medication for Jay when he was two. We tried it only for a short time because the medication only made Jay sleepy.

The neurologist at Kennedy wanted to find a drug that would calm Jay down, help him to focus. Given the controlled environment, I was willing to try again.

The first drug prescribed was Mellaril, a low-potency anti-psychotic commonly used to treat patients with schizophrenia. Jay's behavior didn't change significantly either at home or at school, except that the drug made him lethargic. After about six weeks we stopped it.

The neurologist then prescribed Thorazine, another anti-psychotic used to treat schizophrenia and behavior problems. The results were the same, so again we stopped the drug. We checked those medications off our list of treatment considerations.

Watching the educational and medical professionals work with Jay, and seeing the results, was gratifying. They listened to my fears, concerns and opinions, consulting me on all decisions. And no one judged me.

We became particularly close to Jay's preschool teacher, Cindy, who played a significant role in his life at Kennedy. She hugged him, tickled him and cajoled him into responding to her requests. With Cindy he learned to identify colors, to name and draw a circle, square and triangle, and to count to ten.

When Jay began at Kennedy, he could identify objects and make his basic needs known with single words and a few multiple-word phrases. Through speech therapy, he learned verbs as well as pronouns. Personal pronouns – I, me, mine – seem especially difficult for autistic children to grasp. If I showed Jay a picture of himself and asked who it was, he would invariably say, "That is Jay Fitz," rather than, "That is me."

He often echoed words. If I said, "You are such a good boy," he would repeat, "You are such a good boy." Instead of, "I want to go out," he would say, "you want to go out," again, speech patterns typical of children with autism.

He began to develop more phrases. "Want big brown cookie." "Throw big ball up high." He even learned to procrastinate at bedtime with, "Want drink of water." He began to use adjectives, "Little tiny baby" and "Deep water."

While Jay's speech still sounded stilted, it was mostly functional and at times almost conversational. Rocking contentedly in the front seat during our rides to and from school when children could ride in the front seat untethered, he'd exclaim, "tall tall pole," or "see the moon," two of his favorite things, while flapping and making his EEEEEEE sound. If I failed to respond, he'd put his hands on either side of my face and try to turn my head away from the road, so I'd acknowledge what he had said.

One evening when I was getting Jay ready for bed at home, I tucked the blanket around his tiny chest and shoulders and said, "I love you," and kissed his forehead.

For the first time ever, Jay said "I love you" right back!

I climbed onto the bed with him. "I love you so much, Jay. You are the best boy in the whole world." Overwhelmed with emotion, I wondered if he understood what he had just said.

Jay's increasing ability to communicate and find comfort with his environment gradually had an impact on his behavior. The word "no" replaced tantrums. Mealtimes were more enjoyable, as at Kennedy he learned to eat just about anything. I had to watch him like a hawk, though, as he would dash away without any sense of fear or danger.

Weekend trips to Kennedy developed into a comfortable routine. Our time at home with Jay was filled with family activities intertwined with extended therapy. We still did speech work at the kitchen counter. He spent holidays with us: a week at Thanksgiving and again at Christmas, weeks interspersed through the winter, and extended time on the Cape in the summer.

Our family life settled into a new routine as well. I started teaching in a preschool in Old Deerfield, a small historic village next to Greenfield. Allison began first grade and Betsy fourth, so after getting the girls off to school I headed a couple of miles outside of town to work from 8:30 to noon.

At the preschool I became reacquainted with an old high school friend who also had two little girls, one who had attended dance class with Allison. At the time we were both pregnant, with coinciding due dates. I lost track of her after our boys were born and the dance classes were over. It was a poignant moment to discover that her son, also named Jay, was enrolled in my class. How differently our lives had unfolded since those days before our "Jays" were born.

Did I long for the kind of normalcy her family seemed to enjoy? Did I wish my Jay could be in my little preschool class? Did I feel guilty teaching her child while mine was in the hands of others? All of these questions could be answered with a resounding "yes." I needed to come to terms with my decisions, choices made for the good of my son. A day didn't go by that these struggles didn't enter my mind.

Still I knew that *my* Jay was in the best place for him. Just look at the progress he's making, I reminded myself, and look how well things are going at home with the rest of the family.

Yet disasters can happen even in the most controlled environments. During the spring, one of the cleaning staff left a bottle of lye soap on a hall floor. Fixated on cylinders, Jay spotted the bottle, picked it up and drank some of the poisonous contents. He was rushed to the emergency room on the grounds to have his stomach pumped.

A staff member called that evening to tell me what had happened. Jay was fine, but the news took my breath away. The incident could have resulted in tragedy, and I wasn't there to protect my baby. I hadn't lived up to my promise, "I'll watch over you in my heart."

When I picked up Jay that weekend I was full of questions. "How could this have happened? Why do you use such toxic products? How could someone leave something so dangerous in the reach of children?" Once home, I was ambivalent about bringing him back.

"We've got to speak with the staff," I said to Frank. So I made an appointment to return with Jay, but I wasn't sure I would leave him.

"Look how well he's doing," the director reminded us. "And all poison soaps have been replaced with safer products."

The assurances were not enough, so we spoke with Jay's teacher, Cindy.

"They have all the staff people jumping through hoops regarding safety," she told us. "Jay is as safe here as he would be any place. And you know how I feel about him."

If I took him away, what would I take him home to? The new law mandated services for all special needs youngsters, but the Greenfield school system had devoted few resources to early identification and intervention. The dialogue with the Greenfield School Department remained a constant frustration:

"Mary, we are doing the best we can."

"Mary, we're trying to identify other children to form a program for Jay."

"Mary, the facility we thought might work is not available."

"Mary, we can't . . ."

"Mary, we don't . . ."

I wanted to put my fingers in my ears and hum. I had heard the words too often. They hurt my ears, and my heart.

As much as I wanted Jay home, I wasn't willing to compromise his progress by bringing him home to a poorly organized, ill-conceived curriculum. He was doing too well. But Jay's year at Kennedy was winding down, and more tough choices loomed.

LESSON 13

*When the time comes to let go, weigh your
options and keep a vigilant eye.*

Chapter 14

Frustration

If Jay develops functional speech by five, he has a good chance of catching up to his peers.

Those golden words had tarnished. While Jay had limited functional speech at almost six, and was learning colors, numbers and other skills typical of a five-year-old, developmentally and emotionally he was a long way from "catching up to his peers."

Asked to sit down, he needed assistance to comply. Asked the colors of objects, he would respond but lose interest quickly. He still flapped, rocked and hummed, tuning out the world, requiring one-on-one guidance to maintain focus on a task. He wasn't ready for a mainstream classroom, and classrooms were in no way equipped to deal with his needs.

With the year at Kennedy coming to an end and still no option in Greenfield, we needed to find another quality program. A therapist at Kennedy suggested Spaulding Youth Center in Tilton, New Hampshire. The school was three hours from Greenfield, but had all the components – a behavioral-based curriculum incorporated into the academic and therapeutic programs. At first the Greenfield School Department officials balked at the cost, but after visiting the school and acknowledging they had nothing even close to offer, they agreed that Spaulding was a good choice for Jay.

Adjacent to Interstate 93 in the foothills of New Hampshire's White Mountains, Spaulding Youth Center consists of 470 bucolic wooded acres. One of the oldest child-care facilities in the nation, Spaulding's roots date back to 1871. Responding over the years to the changing needs of children in the New England area, today the school offers round-the-clock treatment to boys and girls ages six to twenty with autism and other neurological impairments.

In the early 1970s Spaulding opened one of the first behavioral-based programs in the country for children with autism. In 1975 the autism program was just two years old, providing services to seven boys ranging in age from six to thirteen. Housed in its own newly-renovated building on the Spaulding campus, the autism unit contained a dormitory-style bedroom, a spacious living area, an eat-in kitchen and a schoolroom.

As the children progressed academically, they were offered the opportunity to attend one of the well-equipped, regular campus classrooms, an intramural mainstream concept. Like the professionals at Kennedy, the staff at Spaulding had high expectations for Jay.

But Spaulding was an even greater distance from home than Kennedy, so we created a new schedule, picking Jay up every other Friday and returning him to school on Sunday. Because of Frank's work schedule, I generally did the pickup and he the return trip.

While Jay handled the return reasonably well, he sometimes cried and asked to come home again, a reflection of his growing emotional development and attachment to his family. Frank remembers many long Sunday evening drives looking at the road through his own tears.

But we saw positive changes in every aspect of Jay's development. On the Saturday of his second weekend home we cleaned the garage, and he stayed right there with us, pointing to objects and naming them, saying things like, "Mommy clean, Daddy break wood." He then went for a ride on the back of Betsy's bike. We still had to watch him assiduously, but he was more eager to be around us.

One Saturday afternoon later that fall I took him for a haircut, an event that used to be a nightmare, requiring one person holding and another snipping. Now sitting calmly in the barber's chair, he looked to his left and then to his right, noticing the mirrors on either side creating reflections. "I see ten Mommies and ten Jay Fitzes," he happily reported.

Numbers seemed to resonate with Jay, and he would often count pillows, toys or other objects. He was also learning to read simple words and phrases.

On a Sunday in late spring as we prepared to drive to Spaulding, he said, "I love you so much. I want to stay home please."

I knew for sure at that moment he knew the meaning of, "I love you." His words overwhelmed me.

That summer Jay spent three separate weeks with us at home and at the Cape. But we moved into fall without any option for him in Greenfield. Again the director said no other children with compatible needs had been found, and an individual program for him would be impossible.

As summer wound down, one of the Spaulding teachers brought Jay home to discuss his future with the County

Collaborative. Pam gave an honest and glowing summary of Jay's progress.

"Why make a change if he's doing so well?" the Greenfield special ed director asked.

While I wanted Jay home desperately, I knew the best opportunity for him was at Spaulding. We agreed with that decision, but in the meantime a woman from the Collaborative would aggressively look for children in other towns with similar needs. Though frustrated, I thought at least we had a plan.

LESSON 14

Frustration is part of the landscape. Trudge on.

Chapter 15

Will They Ever Say They're Sorry?

J ay's chart lay on the counter along with those of his sisters. It was May 1976, and we were at the doctor's office for the children's annual physicals. Our family practitioner and friend had been called out of the exam room.

I reached out to touch Jay, my son who intermittently rocked and hummed, a-six-year-old child with autism. Again his chart caught my eye. With an uneasy feeling of righteous invasion, I opened it.

If there were entries about weight, height and immunizations, I didn't see them. Instead my eyes zeroed in on a series of letters, communications among three physicians: our family practitioner, Dr. D at Mass General and the Medical Director of the Mental Health Center where Jay had been seen years earlier.

My eyes raced through the letters, landing on one written by Jay's physician to his former partner dated March 15, 1972, shortly after we had become involved at the Center.

I was blindsided. After addressing Jay's autism, his physician launched into a character assessment of Frank and me. The words shot off the page like poison arrows, piercing my already fragile being.

"The father, Frank, strikes me as an immature young man. . . heavy reliance on weekend parties . . . excess use of beer. Mary . . . tends to be somewhat flighty . . . I suspect deserts the children for social activities."

The words were impossible to absorb. They didn't describe my world.

My world was overwhelmed with psychologists, speech therapists and social workers.

"Deserts the children?" My world consisted of long days of intense home therapy, teaching Jay to find comfort in his uncomfortable world. "Flighty?" My world was one of research, phone calls, letters and conferences, a world of heart-wrenching decisions.

I had taken all three children to this doctor, listening with pride as he discussed their growth and development. I'd come to that office with ear infections, colds, cuts. I'd also come with a son who was different. From this physician I had desperately sought answers to so many unanswerable questions.

His casting blame on Frank and me only intensified my pain. Worse, it fueled my self-doubt. Without a word about it to the doctor, I left the office feeling utterly betrayed.

As soon as I got home I called Frank at work. "How could the doctor have said such things?" I cried, choking on my words.

Frank was angry, but he remained calm. "Hang on, Mary," he answered. "I'll be right home."

Refusing to believe that we were in any way responsible for Jay's autism, Frank said, "Remember we have two healthy children, raised in the same environment as their brother." I clung to his certainty, seesawing between doubt and determination.

The letter was almost impossible to talk about except with Frank, but I did discuss it with one close friend whose husband happened to be a lawyer.

Her eyes showed the depth of her outrage. "Why would he say such terrible things?" she said. "I thought you were friends."

"So did I. I don't know what to do, and yet I can't stand his ungrounded judgments being part of Jay's file."

"You may have grounds for a lawsuit." She suggested I talk to her husband.

Frank called him that evening. Rather than taking a litigious route, he counseled us to meet face-to-face with each physician. "It's important," he said "to express your feelings directly to each of them."

I first made an appointment with Jay's doctor under the guise of wanting to discuss health issues. We were prepared to demand a copy of the letter and to be tough, even though approaching our family practitioner in an adversarial manner was counterintuitive.

In retrospect, I realize that my relationship with Jay's doctor had been changing over the years. During office visits when I volunteered status reports on Jay's development in other arenas – schooling, social growth, emotional development – he remained distant with no words of encouragement. In a May 1973 journal entry, I observed that he never inquired about Jay when we ran into him at social events.

I wanted to tell him about Jay's progress because we *were* making progress. I wanted him to believe in me when self-doubt was a constant companion. His connection to Jay and me clearly shifted.

Armed with a fierce commitment to my son and a fragile belief in myself, I went to the office with Frank. It should have been comfortable, neutral territory with a few toys and children's books. I often had read aloud to the children until the doctor was ready for us, thinking I was waiting not only for a doctor, but for a friend.

This was a different kind of visit, and the calm escaped me. All that was familiar looked foreign and threatening. My anxiety mixed with rage. We were not waiting for a friend.

Jay's doctor was surprised to see Frank, who had never been to his office. I got straight to the point. "Last week I read a letter in Jay's file, a letter you wrote to the Medical Director at the Mental Health Center several years ago, saying terrible things about us. I'd like to see it again, so both Frank and I can read it."

Stone-faced, he retrieved the file, took out the letter and read it in silence. When he looked up, I put out my hand.

He gave it to me. No reaction, no words, no sensitivity toward us, no remorse. His eyes steeled and his jaw tightened. An apology wouldn't be forthcoming. After reading the letter again, I broke the silence. "Why did you write such things about us?"

He said the psychiatrist at the Mental Health Center had requested information about us after we visited the Center. He had maintained a degree of professional closeness with his former partner. "It's easy for psychiatrists to focus on the positive side of a situation," he said. "I thought he needed help with the negative."

"Why was it necessary to offer negatives? I implored.

He just stared.

His unscientific excuse for his judgment of us made no sense at all. I asked for a copy of the letter and he complied, but we didn't ask that it be removed from Jay's records. I simply took the copy, knowing we'd never had a friend in this man.

A few days later, we met with the psychiatrist at the Mental Health Center. I realized that Dr. K, the young psychologist who had worked with us at the Center must have read the letter too. I also suspected the intern from Hampshire College was privy to it, given her questions about my parenting.

When the psychiatrist finished reading he looked up and said, "I'm sorry to say I don't remember this."

Perhaps. It had been four years since he had received it.

"I want the letter removed from Jay's file," I demanded. "Such negative, inaccurate information may have a negative impact on Jay's future evaluations, on our ability to secure the best help for him."

He listened with apparent compassion. "I'd like to keep the letter in the file with an addendum approved by both of you," he countered, "to use as a learning device for students."

He subsequently mailed the addendum to us, assuring us that the letter would go no further with our names on it. He wanted to use the case anonymously to highlight the importance of accurate communication, the need to filter such reports professionally.

It seemed a reasonable request. Yet a disturbing part of the addendum stated, "In general the effect of parenting in the causation of autistic children has been overplayed in the past. Within the field now, some kind of biogenic or neurologic factors are considered the predominant sources of autism."

Effect of parenting overplayed? Some kind of biogenic or neurologic factors predominant? The medical sentiments of the day still could not relieve parents of responsibility for the disorder. The professionals just couldn't let go of it, and neither could I. What could I say? They were the experts. Their opinions didn't hurt Jay but they killed me.

After those meetings in 1976, I made the following entry in my journal: "The children now see a young pediatrician with whom I've shared our misadventure – case closed! But I'm left with bitterness and distrust which I must work out myself."

I attached the letter to my journal, closed it and never made another entry. Nor did I read my journal again for another thirty years.

Bruno Bettelheim, a promulgator of the "refrigerator mother" theory, committed suicide in 1990. In 1997, the mother of an autistic daughter reviewed two books about him. At the end of the piece titled *In the Case of Bruno Bettelheim*, Molly Finn muses: "It is hard not to speculate about Bettelheim's thoughts as he reviewed his life. In *The Uses of Enchantment*, drawing the moral of a fairy tale, he wrote: 'A voice used to tell lies leads us only to perdition . . . but a voice used to repent, to admit our failures and state the truth, redeems us.' "

Whether or not he repented, it's too late for him to ever say, "I'm sorry."

LESSON 15

*Influential professionals have been dead
wrong in their theories about autism.
Listen to the experts, but don't
succumb to poor judgment.*

Announcing Jay's birth: December 19, 1969

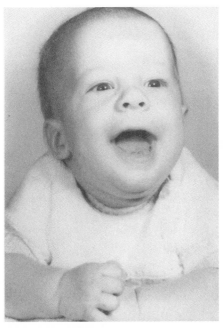

Baby Jay, three months old

The empty film cylinder in Jay's hand saved the day.

Christmas, 1981: age eleven.

A moving picture would have told a different story.

Any cylinder will do.

Four years old.

At age three-and-a-half, with sisters and friends,
wearing his grandfather's first suit (circa 1902).

Poster boy for Project SAVE.,
Spaulding Youth Center, Tilton, NH.

Nine years old. Winter in Maryland.

News Photo: The Howard County Times in Maryland.

Running free. Eleven years old.

Cape Cod, 1978.

Twelve years old.

Jay's artwork: Groden Center
holiday card, 1984.

Special Olympics, 1986.

Betsy's wedding, 1994.

Jay at the helm: Key West, 1998.

The traveling twosome: a three-day,
fun-filled Carnival Cruise.

Growing up: age thirty.

The marketplace in Ajijic, Mexico,
2009.

Chapter 16

The Unexpected

By September 1976 five children had been identified who might benefit from the same type of program Jay needed, and a site was being researched in a small town just east of Greenfield. With a social worker assigned to work with us through Jay's transition to home, I was feeling a little more upbeat.

Yet preparations for Jay's return left me struggling with conflicting emotions. I'd hidden them from everyone, even Frank, but expressed them in my journal: "We had hoped to have Jay home this fall, but he still needs the full-time services at Spaulding. I want him home desperately but am terrified at the same time."

When Jay started at Kennedy, our family developed a comfortable ease of motion in our daily life. Even as I fought for a local education plan, I harbored a quiet fear of Jay's return.

At a meeting that fall at the County Collaborative, I expressed my exasperation over the slow pace of progress. The social worker replied, "A locally-based program isn't the issue right now. You and Frank are not ready to have Jay home."

I was barely able to contain myself. "What do you mean, not ready? How can you make such an outrageous, pat judgment? You've never even been to my house!"

She launched into a lecture about assimilating a special needs child back into the family. Did I know how difficult it would be?

I wish I'd answered, "Yes, but do you?" I wish I'd had the fortitude to admit my fears and say that they were trumped by my need to have him back home.

The decision to send Jay away in the first place was never based on our inability to care for him at home. It was based on the absence of local services. I wanted him back the day after he left. A good, full-day placement for Jay with a strong support system for us was the best possible option. At the same time I was scared to death by the potential challenge of re-entry.

Her judgment cut to my core. Coming just a few months after I read that terrible letter, her assessment added pain to my rage. Neither she nor anyone else from the Collaborative had ever been to our house or seen us interact with our son. Did she believe Jay was better off without his family? Had she been privy to the letter? I was beginning to think that piece of paper was trailing us.

As it turned out, the Cooperative's efforts to create a program failed, and Jay began another year at Spaulding. The autistic unit had received a three-year grant from the U.S. Office of Education, Bureau of Handicapped, to support a new program called S.A.V.E., Study of Autistic Variables in Education. Jay was indeed lucky to be a part of this new approach to finding better ways for autistic children to learn.

As at Kennedy, Jay was the darling of the autistic unit at Spaulding. He became New Hampshire's poster child for autism, his face gracing the covers of brochures for S.A.V.E. and the New Hampshire Society for Autistic Children. Both used a picture of Jay blowing bubbles, delicately holding the wand in one hand while concentrating fiercely on his beautiful bubbles.

During Jay's second year at Spaulding I received a letter from the young woman who had been his teacher the previous year. She had moved to Minneapolis and wrote to find out how Jay was doing, if he had returned home. "I haven't yet found another child quite like Jay," she wrote. Her words brought tears to my eyes.

I took comfort in Jay's progress at Spaulding while we enjoyed our weekends with him at home. But an incident that fall drove home the kinds of challenges we'd face having him home full-time.

Frank was traveling and Jay was home for the weekend with me and his sisters. Late on Saturday afternoon the girls asked to go visit Karen, a favorite babysitter a block from our house. I shouted goodbye from the kitchen thinking they had taken Jay with them as usual. In about an hour they returned – with no Jay.

My heart stopped. First I looked in every corner of the house, under beds, into closets and behind furniture, knowing deep inside my noisy boy was not in the quiet house. I then alerted my neighbors and expanded the search. Frantically I called the police who spread the word through scanners all over town. A legion of total strangers joined the effort.

The eastern edge of Greenfield is bordered by a park and a high wooded ridge we called Rocky Mountain when we were kids. If Jay had followed his sisters and kept going from Karen's house, he would pass through an attractive neighborhood to the park. It has a pond where I skated as a child and trails through the woods over the ridge, a remote piece of country rarely traveled. A dirt road comes out on the other side of the ridge into East Greenfield.

Did Jay go in that direction? Did he fall into the pond? Was he picked up by a stranger? As I was about to lose it, a police officer pulled up to tell me a boy fitting Jay's description had been spotted in East Greenfield, three or four miles from our house. Jay was found walking along, neither alarmed nor frightened.

With darkness falling, he was delivered safely into my arms. I didn't know if I could ever forgive myself, and to this day perhaps I have not. I drove him back to school the next day with my heart still in my mouth.

In November Frank received a call from a silver guild company in Baltimore Maryland, inviting him to apply for a position as Marketing Director with the possibility of becoming Marketing Vice President. Frank had a high regard for the company and believed it offered a good opportunity to move ahead.

Besides uprooting our family, what would a move mean for Jay? What services might be available in Maryland?

Maybe, just maybe, we wouldn't have to wait for a program in Greenfield. Maybe it was time for us to move on.

LESSON 16

Don't fear the unexpected. Sometimes it can provide just what you and your child need.

Chapter 17

Coming Home

Frank went to Baltimore for his first interview at the end of November 1976, returning full of positive, contagious energy. While I was tantalized by the possibilities Baltimore might offer Jay, I was filled with ambivalence.

The move meant leaving family and friends, going into the unknown, abandoning a well-established comfort zone. Yet it might also mean wonderful opportunities for Jay and the girls. Frank and I were more than ready to spread our wings.

I went with Frank for his second interview in January to check out the Baltimore school system for Jay and his sisters. With no illusions that the search would be easy, I hoped Baltimore would offer many more options for Jay.

The people at Spaulding joined in my search. One staff member told me about Linwood Children's Center, a day and boarding school in Howard County, just outside of Baltimore, established exclusively for children with autism. I made an appointment to visit and also scheduled a meeting with a representative from the Baltimore special ed department.

My hope quickly evaporated. The law mandating a "free and appropriate education" for all children with disabilities had been in place barely two years, and the Baltimore school system was teeming with special needs children. The city was still struggling to place them. It could not guarantee that Jay would be placed at Linwood or any school of our choice. Baltimore could become a bureaucratic nightmare. Jay could be lost.

The city's public schools were also faced with over-crowded classrooms, racial tensions and poor test scores. If we chose to settle in Baltimore proper, we would need to consider private school for the girls. Even with Frank's antic-ipated raise, private school didn't compute for us.

Baltimore did not look promising. Frank was completely involved in the interview process, and I found myself alone, navigating a tricky move.

But the more I talked to people, the more I learned about possibilities for Jay. Under the new federal law, if we lived anywhere in Howard County, the county would be responsible for Jay's education, and it had one of the best reputations in the state. With Linwood Children's Center located there, my focus quickly shifted from the city to the suburbs.

I met with Howard County's special education director the next morning, told him about Jay and our interest in Linwood. He said it was the best facility in the state for children with autism. Encouraged, I took the paperwork required by the county for application. Later that day, Frank and I visited Linwood.

Housed in a nineteenth century stone house in Ellicott City, an attractive, historic town in eastern Howard County, Linwood Children's Center served 27 children. It was founded in 1955 by Jeanne Simons, a pioneer in the treatment of autistic children, who had emigrated from the

Netherlands and earned her master's degree in social work from Boston College.

A Linwood social worker told us about the school's history, philosophy and structure. Claire explained that the Linwood method didn't follow a behavioral model. Instead, it focused on the worth of the autistic child as an individual, judging neither parent nor child.

I could feel and see it in the way the staff interacted with the children and with us. Every room buzzed with children engaged in activities geared to their needs. And Miss Simons had a documented track of success with these children. This was the place for Jay.

Driving back to our hotel that afternoon, I told Frank that I thought we should look at houses in Howard County. Jay will be close to home.

Frank agreed. "Let's see what happens with the job, and then I'll look into the commute."

"Are they ready to make an offer?" I asked.

"I'm cautiously optimistic."

That evening we had dinner with a couple of executives and their wives, and the next morning the company made Frank an offer. The terms met our expectations, and Frank accepted. He would start mid-February.

I had turned 180 degrees in 24 hours, from discouragement about Baltimore to excitement about Howard County and Linwood Children's Center. Once back in Greenfield, I completed the application process. Spaulding sent Jay's records, and the two schools shared information. Jay was accepted at Linwood as a day student. He was coming home.

I knew our family's delicate balance was fragile. Bringing Jay home after three years was a victory, a change I'd craved.

Filled with fear, yet pushed by positive prospects, I began to plan for our family's major upheaval.

———

LESSON 17

Sometimes you fear what you most want.
Don't give in to the fear.

Chapter 18

Reunited

The huge truck rumbled out of our driveway in Greenfield on Wednesday, July 20, 1977, filled with all the tangible evidence of who we were and how we lived: furniture, family treasures, photographs and books. We would meet it in two days at our new house in Maryland. As I watched the 18-wheeler drive away, I wondered irrationally – will it be there when we arrive? Its disappearance around the corner intensified my fear.

I walked through all the empty rooms, saying goodbye to the memories . . . the living room that first Christmas Eve with baby Jay, the dining room that Easter with 26 people, the kitchen with Jay rocking frantically to the dishwasher, and his bedroom with scrapes on the floor from his rocking crib. Turning slowly, I walked out the door for the last time, unprepared for the mix of emotions inherent in such a life change.

Frank had moved to a company apartment in February, coming home every other weekend. I stayed in Greenfield with the children so we could all finish out the school year. We'd put the house on the market immediately, and during his weekends in Maryland, Frank looked at houses in Howard County.

Adjacent to the western corner of Baltimore's city limits, Howard County spreads westward for miles. In 1977 most of the land was rolling hills, cornfields and horse farms, with tiny towns nestled in between. Frank figured he would have a commute of 20 to 30 minutes. The commute to Linwood would be even shorter.

During April vacation the girls and I drove to Maryland to look at houses Frank had lined up. We found a newly constructed Cape in a brand new subdivision in the town of Glenwood. We would be going from an old Victorian in the center of a small New England town to a contemporary Cape on an acre in the southern countryside. The "town" was a post office, period. Our Maryland realtor referred to Howard County as God's country. I found it Godforsaken.

Even though we hadn't sold our house in Greenfield, we made an offer. The wheels were in motion.

The girls seemed excited about the move, and we were all pleased to be so close to Washington, DC. Allison would be going into fourth grade and Betsy would start middle school in seventh. They talked about missing their friends without tears or excessive anxiety, which helped me significantly. But the logistics were daunting.

Packing up a twelve-room house is a tremendous task. Getting it all into a house half the size would be impossible. So in late June I had the yard sale of the century, weeding out what would come to Maryland and what would be sold.

"What about the piano?" Frank asked as we tried to make hard decisions. "There's no room for it in the new house."

I had painted the old player piano yellow to match the walls in a sunny room on the south side of the house, and we had many fun gatherings with friends standing around singing old tunes cranked off from the player rolls. I suggested we take it anyway. Maybe we could put it in the basement.

The piano made the cut, but many other items of sentimental value found their way into the yard sale. I went back and forth over my grandmother's crystal – should I sell it or not? I finally did, to the woman across the street. An antique lady's desk went to a stranger. Some things I was glad to get rid of – an old couch, a rickety end table – but as we carted things out to the driveway, each room began to lose its character. We were dismantling eight years of family life.

Once Frank started to work in Baltimore, I talked to Jay about our move every time he was home. I explained that he would no longer live at Spaulding, that he would go to a new school and live at home.

He seemed to understand to some extent, but I know the idea of his entire family moving to a new place confused him. He had never lived anywhere but the house in Greenfield.

We decided to make the initial move without Jay, take two weeks to unpack and get organized before bringing him to Maryland. The beautiful warm day we said good-bye to in Massachusetts was blisteringly hot in the southern countryside. Luckily our new house had central air, and for two weeks I unpacked while the girls made friends in the neighborhood.

At the end of those two weeks, with the house reasonably well-settled, we headed to New Hampshire to pick up Jay. On our way we stopped in Greenfield for Sally, our babysitter who would spend the summer with us. From Spaulding we all drove to the Cape for a week, then to our new home in Maryland. Home with our son. A family reunited.

LESSON 18

*Every major move with an autistic child
requires sensitivity and a plan.
Plan well.*

Chapter 19

Our Own Normal

Our house in Maryland was twelve miles from Ellicott City and the nearest supermarket. The lot backed up to a cornfield near the end of a dead-end street in a new subdivision full of young families with lots of children.

At the bottom of our new driveway, along the side of the road, was a newly installed, open-ended drain pipe – a perfect cement cylinder – for Jay a bit of Nirvana. Pipes just like it had been installed throughout the neighborhood to divert rainwater from the road, and Jay discovered ours in a flash. If I turned my back for a second, he tore down the driveway to his newest treasure.

Sometimes he ran joyfully from one end to the other, EEEEEing. Other times he just stood and rocked from side to side to the rhythms playing in his head. Though the pipes were dry and new, I was terrified when I couldn't see him, so whenever he headed for the pipe, I put him in his room. Behavior therapy was still part of my arsenal, but it was no match for cylinders. "I do like the drainpipe, Mummy," he insisted.

Jay's other favorite objects were his "jeep truck toys." He gathered the small, plastic, green army jeeps in a bag or lined them up on the floor in his bedroom. He also fixated on a green, plastic toy rifle. His perfect outing was a trip to K-Mart to buy one of the toys or to the hardware store for cylindrical pieces of PVC pipes, followed by lunch at McDonalds.

Jay also was captivated by hot air balloons. He looked for pictures of them in magazines, and was always the first to spot one from the car. One early Saturday morning during our first summer in Maryland, we awoke to see the sky in our neighborhood filled with these magical objects. As we all rushed outside, one balloon made an emergency landing right in our own treeless backyard! Flapping and humming, Jay was beside himself, grinning from ear to ear.

"Hey, Jay," I asked as we walked over to take a closer look. "How would you like to go up in the hot air balloon?"

"No, thank you," he replied.

"Aw, c'mon, Jay," I teased. "I'll go up with you."

"No, thank you," he again answered. "It would be too scary." While Jay loved hot air balloons, he hated heights, and the close encounter in our backyard was good enough for him.

Our yard also provided relief from the oppressive Maryland heat. New England is peppered with rivers, ponds and lakes, but the ice age excavation didn't reach as far south as Maryland, and the ocean was miles away from us. Jay discovered the perfect solution – the garden hose. He'd hold the hose in the air and stand under it, letting the cool water course over his body, or wave it in the air watching the water stream form patterns, EEEEEing, flapping, stimming the whole time.

The move seemed to be working out pretty well. Linwood proved a terrific match for Jay. Betsy and Allison made lots of friends, and often took their brother with them to meet kids in the neighborhood. On weekends Frank and I dove into backyard landscaping.

But while some new friends welcomed Jay into their lives, others were not so accepting. One day Allison came in from playing, distressed. "Joey said his father wouldn't let him come near Jay because he would catch what Jay has. Can anybody catch what Jay has?"

"Of course not, honey," I replied. "You know Jay was born with autism. It's not a bad thing. He's just different and some people don't understand."

While calmly reassuring Allison, I was raging inside, thinking of the Rogers and Hammerstein song from South Pacific:

You've got to be taught before it's too late,
Before you are six or seven or eight,
To hate all the people your relatives hate,
You've got to be carefully taught!

Joey was being carefully taught, and I was furious. The impact of such ignorance was assuaged somewhat by the steadfast kindness and understanding of others.

Part of me was still struggling with the move. In Greenfield I had been intimately involved with a small, self-contained community. In the Maryland countryside I often felt isolated and lonely, and had trouble feeling like it was home. While driving to the market one day, I experienced a kind of epiphany as a funeral cortege passed: people are born here and die here. This is a real place. Yet I felt as if I were in suspended animation, waiting to land where I really belonged.

Fall brought some order. The girls liked their schools, and I got involved with the Parents Association at Linwood, where I met other parents facing challenges similar to ours. I also met a woman who became my running partner.

A daily rhythm emerged. Betsy and Allison took the school bus in front of our house every morning, and a small bus picked Jay up each day at the end of the driveway. As soon as the kids were off, my running friend and I hit the pavement.

One weekday morning in October I took Jay to a doctor's appointment in Ellicott City, and then to McDonalds for lunch before taking him to school. As we passed a table where an older couple was eating, Jay blithely helped himself to a French fry. The woman's face went from surprise to distinct displeasure. I apologized profusely, attempting to explain Jay's special needs. But how many times have you felt like doing that very thing when your stomach grumbles and the deliciously greasy smell of French fries wafts through the air?

I pulled Jay aside and spoke to him quietly. "Jay, we have to wait for our own food. The food on other tables is not for us. Let's go over and say you're sorry."

"I am sorry. Thank you," he said to the woman in his polite monotone. I took his hand and gave it a squeeze, stifling a laugh as we walked away.

On another trip to Ellicott City, an obese woman stood in the checkout line just ahead of us in K-Mart. Her bottom, tightly encased in pink elastic, was right at Jay's eye level, and I could see he was intrigued. Before I could stop him, he poked his forefinger into her backside. Momentarily horrified, I pretended not to notice as we paid our bill and rushed out of the store. When we got in the car I burst out laughing, thinking of the Pillsbury doughboy. We had a little talk about not touching strangers.

We were settling in. Temper tantrums had become almost non-existent. The previous year Spaulding reported that Jay resorted to tantrums "when he couldn't get his own way," implying he was acting like a spoiled child. I believe the tantrums were the result of his having neither the verbal skills nor the emotional development to express his needs. As he became more verbal, the outbursts diminished. His speech remained a monotone, but was clear and effective.

The Linwood method contained many elements of Jay's previous programs, and he responded well. According to The Hidden Child; The Linwood Method for Reaching the Autistic Child, "The Linwood approach to shaping behavior relies on positive reinforcement of aspects of existing behaviors rather than an aversive conditioning or punishment." We completely embraced the Linwood Method.

Jay's hyperactivity and stimming persisted, as did some of his destructive behaviors toward objects and himself. His beautiful front teeth had come in, big and protruding, but he banged them to the point where he eventually broke off the tips.

We found a wonderful pediatric dentist who determined that Jay needed to have four back teeth extracted, followed by a regimen of orthodontics and caps on his front teeth when he was older. The extractions were done under general anesthesia, and Jay tolerated them well.

"I was so so brave," Jay announced proudly after the procedure. And he was brave – an excellent patient.

Through Linwood, Jay learned to swim at the Ellicott City YMCA. We joined a swim and tennis club where the girls competed on the swim team. On weekends at the pool, Jay jumped endlessly into the deep end, scrambling in and out of the water. I had to drag him away before he got waterlogged.

One August when swim team was over, we spent a week visiting friends in Vermont, hiking and camping in New Hampshire's White Mountains. Jay loved to ride in the car, so the trip proved exhilarating for him. Whenever we started off on a family adventure, we all sang "We're off to see the wizard, the wonderful wizard of Oz," and Jay joined in with toneless enthusiasm.

By this time, he had already developed his uncanny understanding of geography and sense of direction. He knew right off which was north, south, east or west. When he rode in the car, he rocked to his own cadence, asking periodically what state we were in or what bridge we were crossing.

We traveled through New Jersey and into New York State, through the soft contours of the Catskills and into Vermont. We visited friends in Manchester and then drove to Lake Dunmore where I had summered with my family as a child. Leaving Vermont, we crossed the Connecticut River into New Hampshire, heading to the majestic White Mountains.

Hiking up Mt. Washington, Jay's stamina amazed us. Only ten years old, he led the charge up the steep, rocky trail.

"What a 'biew!'" he exclaimed every time he stopped for a few seconds.

What a good decision it was to bring Jay home where we could guide his growth and development. His good nature was becoming more and more apparent. And while he still didn't like to be touched, he allowed me to hug him – gently. No more French fry incidents. We were finding our own version of normal.

During our fourth and final year in Maryland, I took a fifth-grade teaching position at a private country day school where we enrolled Allison. Betsy started her freshman year at a private high school in Baltimore County. With Jay at Linwood, we were all "well placed." It could have been a perfect year.

But Frank's company was sold and he was squeezed out, verbal promises never honored. He found a position with a silver company in Connecticut and moved there alone while we made plans to join him in June. That job didn't work out: another blow, creating financial and emotional strain. Ultimately he found a new opportunity in Providence, Rhode Island, so plans for another move were put into place.

As the beautiful cherry blossoms erupted in Washington D.C. in the spring of 1981, thoughts of moving to Rhode Island filled my head with new possibilities. I still considered New England home, and we'd be an hour and a half from Cape Cod, family and friends. We were thrilled, but most important were the options for Jay.

Years before at a conference on autism, I had learned of Rhode Island's Behavioral Development Center, a school for autistic children founded by Drs. June and Gerry Groden. The Grodens were pioneers in the study and treatment of autism, so I set my sights on what looked like an exceptional placement for Jay.

Frank started work in Providence on June 1, 1981. I followed with the children in August after closing on the house in Maryland. I felt a sense of peace that night on the road, making our last trip from Maryland to Rhode Island. We spent the night in a motel in Delaware in one room with two double beds and a cot, a family living and moving as one.

How could I possibly know of the heartbreak to come?

———

LESSON 19

Don't forget to laugh.

Chapter 20

Promises Made—
Promises Broken

In the spring of 1981, we found a four-bedroom house in Barrington, a shore community less than half an hour from Frank's new office in Providence and a block from Narragansett Bay, in the path of southwest breezes off the water all summer long. We moved into our home ready to embrace the joys of beachside living.

Barrington had an excellent school system, and during one of my first visits, I met with the newly appointed Director of Special Education. I described Jay's disabilities and the services he'd been receiving. The Special Ed Director was skeptical. "We'll need to do an evaluation to determine the diagnosis," he said. "We want to make sure he's properly placed."

"Jay's almost twelve years old," I insisted. "He's been diagnosed with autism through physicians and schools. The issue is not diagnosis, but proper services."

"That won't be easy. The Barrington school system has a special needs classroom," he explained, "but no services targeted specifically to autism."

I suggested that the Behavioral Development Center (BDC) in Providence would be the perfect solution. I had just met with Dr. June Groden and toured the Center. The program was beyond my wildest dreams, and I desperately wanted Jay to have that opportunity.

In June I brought Jay to an evaluation with the Special Ed Director in Barrington and for an intake interview at BDC. Everyone acknowledged that he was autistic and that the special needs classroom in Barrington would not be an appropriate option. He started at BDC in August, the week after we moved, the type of placement I once thought only a tantalizing dream. According to the law, the town of Barrington funded his tuition.

A small yellow school bus picked him up each morning. The driver was an irrepressible woman who embraced her charges as if they were her own children. At 3:30 every afternoon, Lulu returned Jay safely to the doorstep.

We took out a family membership at the Barrington YMCA, and I started running with new friends. Our house became a hub of activity with the girls' friends coming and going. Our family seemed settled once again.

But things were not as they appeared. Something began to eat at me. Frank showed little interest in intimacy, and at first I thought it must be his new job and long hours. It had never been his habit to work late, but now he often worked until after 7:00 pm. He had made the move ahead of us, living in an apartment in Providence for two-and-a-half months, setting his own schedule.

Living in a new community with few friends and three young children was hard, but not unusual for the wife of a young executive. Gradually Frank's 7:00 pm return began to slip toward 8:00. Sometimes I called to see when he'd be home for dinner, and usually found him in his office. Though confused and worried, I felt guilty bothering him.

As early fall crept toward holiday time, Frank distanced himself more and more from me. We invited extended family for Thanksgiving to celebrate our return to New England. The day was filled with holiday fun but with one mishap: I'd forgotten to put the turkey in the oven.

Sitting outside on the back steps, the turkey was out of sight, out of mind. It was almost noon when I remembered, and that 20 pounder was going to take some time. But dinner just turned out to be a little later than planned, and all was well. . . I thought.

As everyone was leaving that evening, Frank's mother pulled me aside to say that Frank seemed unusually quiet and withdrawn. Hearing my inner concerns expressed by someone else took me aback. When our guests left, I asked over and over what was wrong, but got no answer. By Christmas he was becoming morose. What the hell was wrong?

Frank wasn't interested in going out New Year's Eve, so I suggested a quiet evening at home. Betsy was spending the night with a friend. Allie and Jay ate early and got into their pajamas. Allie went up in our bedroom to watch TV and wait for the ball to drop in Times Square while Jay hung out until bedtime.

I had bought lobsters and wine for a special dinner-for-two, champagne for midnight. I started a fire in the living room fireplace and set the dining room table with candles. By 7:30 when Frank had not come home, I began to worry. At 8:00, I called his office and got no answer. I tucked Jay in around 8:30 – still no Frank. Just before 9:00, he came through the door carrying a half empty six-pack of beer.

"Where have you been?" I tried to keep my voice unemotional.

"Having a couple of beers with friends." His tone was angry.

Doubts began to roar in my head. "Were you with a woman?"

"No," he shouted. "I told you I was with friends!"

The gut-wrenching confrontation ended with me in tears, begging for the truth. But he didn't want to talk and retreated to the living room. Angry, hurt and frustrated, I drove alone to a nearby mall and saw a movie, returning home after 2:00 am. Everyone was asleep. New Year's Eve had come and gone. The next morning, I tossed the lobsters.

In the days that followed, every attempt I made to talk escalated into a fight. He told me to "stop beating a dead horse." Bruised, I backed off.

The following Friday we went to a movie and then stopped at a local pub for a beer. It was a perfect time and place to talk, so I told him I wanted to see a marriage counselor, as I was struggling with the terrible problem between us.

"See a psychologist? Better be careful," he replied indignantly. "In Rhode Island anyone can hang out a shingle and call himself a therapist."

"How do you know that?" I asked. "You've never had any experience with therapy."

"A friend in my office told me."

"A friend in your office? Who would you talk to in your office about something so personal?" I struggled to remain calm.

And then the bottom fell out. He just let go, with a slight grin, almost as if he couldn't wait to tell me. He had been seeing a woman since June named Hedi. By the time I got to Rhode Island in August, the affair was in full swing. My world suddenly crystalized, then shattered into minute particles and evaporated. I slipped from the bar stool, went to the ladies room and threw up.

The next day Betsy and Allison were off with friends. Frank had just left for a business meeting in Atlantic City and I was standing over my kitchen sink sobbing when Jay came into the room. Brow furrowed, he said, "Mummy does cry."

I didn't know where to turn. Only in Rhode Island for five months, I had no close friends nearby. None of my old friends was divorced but my sister-in-law, Barrie, had divorced Frank's brother several years before. Though she had remarried, we had remained fast friends through the years.

Rocked to my core, I took the children to her house in Marblehead to spend the rest of the weekend. I was moving into the eye of a raging tempest with no rudder and no compass. Barrie listened patiently. She tried to comfort me with words, backrubs and jokes. I was not to be comforted, and I knew I needed help.

When I returned home I called June Groden, the only psychologist I knew. Frank and I met together and individually over the next several weeks with a therapist she suggested, but Frank told me after one meeting he stopped to see Hedi on the way home. One evening, driving home alone from a joint session, I found myself speeding carelessly.

Over too much wine and beer when my brother's wife was visiting, conversation turned to Hedi. Sandy made derogatory remarks, baiting Frank, singing, "Hedi, Hedi, Hedi." Frank got his back up, warning her to be quiet. I diffused the situation before it got ugly, insisting we all go to bed.

When we got upstairs to our bedroom, I felt a visceral need for my husband, hating him, but wanting him desperately. My body craved him, and the alcohol tempered his inhibitions. We made love. Or had sex. The next morning a sullen man told me he felt guilty for cheating on his lover.

In March I told Frank I wanted him to move out. Having him in the house, right there for me to touch, was a kind of purgatory. Early on a Saturday morning in April, we drove to New Bedford to run a half-marathon with some Y friends. As we started to run, a public address system blasted the celebratory piece from <u>Chariots of Fire</u>. It seemed the music was playing for Frank's departure – a stirring send-off. He left the next day.

I took the children to Barrie's, leaving Frank to pack. Jay pooped on Barrie's bedroom floor, the sort of thing he hadn't done since he was three years old. Once again, he was unable to express his emotions verbally.

Returning late Sunday evening, we came into a house devoid of Frank, not even a phone number or address. Jay raced through the hall, grabbed my mother's beautiful antique doll and flung it to the floor. The bisque head exploded into a million pieces – like my life. I knelt down and picked up delicate fragments. It was broken beyond repair.

Later I stood alone in my kitchen with <u>Chariots of Fire</u> raging in my head. We were a family devastated by betrayal. Both my mother's doll and my children were collateral damage.

The person I loved had disappeared. I felt used and discarded, replaced. The sturdy warrior was slipping away.

How would I take care of my children alone? How would I cope with Jay? How would I survive? I wasn't sure I wanted to.

LESSON 20

Don't be afraid or ashamed to reach out for help.

Chapter 21

From a Cauldron of Despair

In May, 1982, the cherry tree outside our bedroom began to flower in wonderful shades of purple, pink and white. My husband would never share this sight with me. He was gone.

The pain had become physical. My heart was heavy every waking moment. I couldn't eat or sleep well. During a couple of runs with friends, I stopped and threw up.

Friends and acquaintances had varied reactions. A neighbor who had befriended us as a couple when we first moved to Barrington stopped calling. One summer day I heard a group of women chatting and laughing on her porch, a luncheon party that didn't include me. The realtor who had sold us the house called to invite us for dinner. When I told her Frank and I had separated, she laughed nervously. I never heard from her again.

Though there were miles between us, my old friends in Greenfield remained true. A couple of them came to stay with me for a few days at a time. They called often and took my calls any time of day or night. My former sister-in-law, Barrie, was an ever-present support.

The most important person to intervene on my behalf was June Groden. I had no job, and I needed one, but Rhode

Island wasn't hiring teachers. June said she needed someone at BDC to do PR and fundraising, and asked if I'd come on board part-time.

"I have no experience in that field, June. I wouldn't know where to begin."

June flattered me. "You're articulate, smart and organized. Put those qualities to work for us at the Center."

With my self-esteem at zero, I didn't like the person living inside me and needed to make a change. Gratefully accepting her compliments and her offer, I started at BDC in late January.

I liked the work. The hours filled with tasks took my mind from my torment, and the contact with people was a tonic. Honing my photography and writing skills, I produced a slide show and took it out to the community. I wrote press releases and a direct-mail solicitation letter. I also took on menial tasks, everything from stuffing envelopes to answering the phone.

The Behavioral Development Center also turned out to be a perfect fit for Jay. I felt I had a whole team, a large, multidisciplinary, dedicated group of professionals who wanted to help youngsters like Jay and had the skills to do it. I loved talking to the public about what an extraordinary place it was. I also loved being there, a part of Jay's life on a day-to-day basis.

When Jay started at BDC, he was still a little boy, small for his eleven years at fifty-three inches and sixty-three pounds. While his progress was steady, his behaviors could still be destructive and at times dangerous.

He liked to climb the pine tree in front of our house to "see a biew." His father or I had to coax him down each time, as the branches were too small for us to climb up after him. His flapping persisted as did his staring at lights and shadows. Throwing, biting and hair-pulling erupted occasionally.

He started to grab at women's chests. I knew it wasn't a sexual gesture. When I asked why, he replied, "Because I do like the shape of a cone."

Cylinders remained his favorites, and he developed a fixation on cylindrical water towers. He also began to swear, and rituals such as hand-washing and teeth-tapping remained a part of his repertoire.

But he responded extremely well to the direct behavioral approach at BDC. With intervention, the breast-grabbing and the swearing stopped. He corrected anyone who swore in his presence saying, "Oh shoot, shoot, shoot is right, right, right." A veritable arbiter of appropriate language he became!

An entry in his school records read, "Jay has made excellent progress during the past year. His behavior has improved markedly, and he is less hyperactive and exhibits fewer inappropriate behaviors." All that was well-documented in charts at school was evident at home as well.

At Christmastime that year Jay learned to sing "Oh Christmas Tree." Monotone though it was, we encouraged him to perform often.

Unfortunately my time at BDC was short, as I needed a full-time job. In early March a friend saw an ad in the Providence Journal for a job with "my name all over it." St. Andrew's School in Barrington was looking for a Director of Development and Public Relations.

We sat on her living room floor and "made up" a resume from what my mother would have called "whole cloth."

Pulling from the fundraising I'd done for the school where I taught in Maryland, as well as my work at BDC, I got myself down on paper.

I hand-delivered the resume to St. Andrew's, a small Episcopal day and boarding school about two minutes from my house. After several interviews, I was offered the job. I finished at BDC on the last Friday in March. On Monday morning, April 1st, shaking in my boots, I began a new career at St. Andrew's School.

Still crawling out of a cauldron of despair, I needed every bit of inner strength to face the challenge. For starters, I had to learn to type. A brand new IBM Selectric sat ominously next to my desk, so I attended a typing class three nights a week. I got home from work, made dinner for the kids and left for class.

Each way in the car I found myself overwhelmed with sadness and fear. Sometimes I sang old church hymns from childhood, a way of praying, I suppose.

Abide with me; fast falls the eventide.

The darkness deepens; Lord with me abide. . .

The words were choked with tears. Feeling vulnerable, I talked to my mother as I would have as a little girl. "Mama, are you there? Do you know where I am? Please help me."

During the day I immersed myself in work. Typing was the least of it, as I built an office that would raise millions of dollars over my five-and-a-half years there. St. Andrew's became more than a job. The headmaster and his wife became dear friends who supported me professionally and emotionally as I navigated the path to divorce. They embraced Jay and my girls. Along with others at the school, they offered a sense of community and family.

I hated letting my children see me distraught, but it was impossible to always keep my feelings hidden. In his own way Jay was affected deeply. He didn't know how to react like his sisters, who were also mourning a terrible loss. They sometimes cried when I cried. Other times they hugged me. Sometimes they got angry.

Jay simply didn't have the tools to express himself that way. He didn't know how to sympathize or empathize. Acting out was the only way he released tension and anxiety.

At the same time, the storm of emotions filling our house seemed to provide an emotional learning environment for Jay. I first got a glimpse of it not long after Frank left. Shortly after Easter, my mother-in-law underwent a hip replacement and was laid up for several weeks. One day I drove with Jay to meet my father-in-law at a halfway point to deliver a casserole, flowers and books.

Placing the casserole carefully on the floor of the back-seat near Jay, I cautioned him not to touch the dish with his feet. We stopped for him to go to the bathroom, and he accidentally knocked the dish over. With my nerves shot, I went ballistic, screaming at him. He quietly rocked for a moment and then began to belt out, "Oh Christmas tree, oh Christmas tree, how beautiful and bright."

He knew how happy I was when he sang that song. He was saying, "I'm sorry. I didn't mean to do that. I don't want you to be upset."

Gathering him into my arms, I hugged him and apologized. I managed to scoop most of the casserole back into the dish. No one was any the wiser.

And I saw my son in a whole new light, growing physically and emotionally.

LESSON 21

Fear can be a great motivator.
Don't let it paralyze you

Chapter 22

A Time to Heal

Despair is insidious. It crept into my being, robbing me of both physical and mental energy, waiting to steal my self-esteem. I got help through a short stint with therapy, and sought out quality time with good friends. I needed my sanity for my children, yet I was most vulnerable to this demon when I was at home.

For years I had defined myself as "wife and mother." Now half of that identity was gone. Who cares? I thought. Who do I have to cook for? The kids aren't interested. I stopped making my bed every day and was careless about the house. Grocery shopping became haphazard.

One day when Betsy was home with a couple of friends, one said, "Betsy, why doesn't your mother keep any food in the house?"

Why, indeed? The answer was simple. I was depressed. I didn't have the money for regular visits to a shrink, so my doctor prescribed Ativan, an anti-anxiety drug. It only made me groggy, so I stopped taking it after a couple of weeks.

I wasn't the only one feeling hurt. Each one of us was suffering, and the wounds were raw. Betsy became hyper-critical of me and extremely self-centered. Though money was short, she wanted the best clothes. A high school sophomore in a new school, appearances were important. She found a very expensive prom dress that spring and asked me to come with her to see it. It was way beyond my means, but she insisted, wearing me down, making me feel guilty. I caved and bought the dress.

Her father had moved in with his girlfriend, and initially Betsy wanted nothing to do with them. But at the end of that first summer, she drove to their apartment to confront Hedi. According to Betsy's account, she asked, "What the hell do you think you're doing wrecking our wonderful family?"

I was amazed. Betsy wasn't a confronter. She would usually listen to her father and me, and then do her own thing, rather than argue.

Allison revealed her pain in different ways. From her thirteen-year-old vantage point, she said, "Mom, I thought our family was better than this. This happens to other people."

Getting her to do homework was a nightmare, and her grades began to fall. Allison *was* a confronter, and she confronted me. If I said, "Allie, you look great today," she would answer, "You mean I didn't look good yesterday?" Nothing was right.

I learned the extent of Jay's awareness in an unusual way. He loved to listen to music on the radio, especially in the car where he rocked to the beat. He also knew the names of most songs and the artists, and as time went on he'd tell me the month and year a song came out. One day he asked, "Please change the station, Mummy."

"Why, Jay?"

"Because that is a sad song," he answered.

"Why is it a sad song?"

"Because that is a song from 1982 when Mummy did cry."

He reacted to my sadness, as well as his own, through the music.

During those early months of flying solo I found a therapist who led a more affordable weekly group session with five men and five women, all divorced, separated or widowed, and all in their thirties or early forties. The easy dialogue and common ground offered personal insight as well as welcome social connections.

Occasionally I had a private session with the therapist, and after one meeting, I had a revelation. I came away frustrated with my inability to "feel better." It became clear that I was looking for others to make that happen. While therapy, friends, family, and a short-lived Ativan prescription might be important aspects of my healing, I had to do the work.

The process needed my direction, my control. Like decisions I had made for Jay over the years, I needed to take charge of my own well-being, to resurrect the warrior, to forget what I had lost and celebrate what I had. It was only a beginning, but that awareness was a powerful force.

The mother of one of Allison's good friends had been recently widowed. We became close and often had dinner together on Friday nights at a local restaurant. Over a glass of wine, we talked about how our mothers used to refer to women knocked by adversity as "poor souls."

"No way anyone's going to call me a poor soul," I declared.

"Me neither," Lila agreed.

A pact was made. I felt a new identity emerging.

I was asked to join a newly created Special Education Advisory Committee, aimed at assessing and serving special needs children in the community. On the state level, I served on a committee that was part of the Governor's Council for the Handicapped. These organizations offered unique insight into the workings of the relatively new public law 94-142, and how that mandate should best be implemented for children like Jay. The work also pulled my emotions outward, providing a framework to combat my devastating loss of self-esteem.

With St. Andrew's right across the street from the high school, I was always nearby if the girls needed me. They developed a tight group of friends, good kids who were achievers and athletes, who shared aspirations for college, and whose families cared about where they were and what they were doing. And they were great with Jay.

"Hey, Jay, how're you doing?" the kids asked when they came into the house. They approached him with high-fives, to which he responded with a stilted but sincere, "I am fine, thank you."

Although Jay's speech was improving dramatically, he didn't develop the body language, gestures or facial expressions that typically accompany the development of language. Innuendo and subtle humor were lost on him. But his speech was useful and functional.

He still needed prompting with eye contact and pronouns, and he also tended to repeat. If I asked, "Do you want some milk?" he usually replied, "Want some milk, please," leaving out the personal pronoun and repeating the question, instead of saying, "Yes I do."

On the other hand, his vocabulary was developing

rapidly and he was responsive, especially if he was interested.

"Jay, what shape is the telephone pole?" I'd ask.

He'd respond quickly, "It is a cylinder."

Jay's monotone could be modified if I asked him to imitate me, but he's never truly understood the relationship between words and tone. During a conversation one Christmas while I was wrapping presents, I asked him not to come into the room because there were surprises.

He said, "It is a surprise," without any intonation or use of the contraction.

"Jay," I said, "say 'it's a sur-<u>pri</u>-ise.'" I used the contraction and gave the word surprise three syllables, my voice going up on the middle, accented syllable. To this day, whenever I wrap gifts, he uses the melodic phrase, "It's a sur-<u>pri</u>-ise." He loves surprises and never peeks!

Jay responded well to "what" and "where" questions, but to this day has trouble with "how" and "why." "What star is that in the sky?" I asked. "That is the planet Venus." However, if I asked how he knew, he used the pat answer, "Because I am smart."

He always answered in the concrete, unable to grasp the abstract.

"Hey, Jay, what's up?" I once asked.

"The sky is up, Mummy," he answered.

With his literal pattern of thinking, Jay couldn't lie, as his sisters learned the hard way. It was evident they loved their brother. They looked after him without complaint and included him in social activities when appropriate, and sometimes when inappropriate. Once when Betsy was home from college, she took Jay to a party, and when they came home, I asked him what the kids did at the party.

He replied in his guileless monotone, "They did drink beer."

Though he was simply stating a fact without judgment, Jay perceived alcohol as bad. When he was twelve years old, he took an opened bottle of wine from the refrigerator and drank the whole thing, becoming drunk and sick to his stomach. I cleaned him up and put him in the bathtub and then put him to bed. To this day he will not touch an alcoholic drink.

While Jay's negative behaviors were dissipating significantly, I still needed to watch him closely. We lived on a busy road, but he knew that cars were dangerous. He liked to play in the driveway with his tubes, making up things to do with them. He scraped a piece of a PVC plumbing tube on the macadam, wearing the tube down to a small ring.

He knew not to get close to the road, but I caught him once interlocking drinking straws, making a long tube to push down the driveway to the edge of the road. I also caught him throwing things at moving cars. With the help of the staff at BDC, I implemented a behavior modification program to stop this behavior immediately.

Jay found plenty of other things to keep him occupied at home. His obsession with plastic included blowup beach balls and globes. He blew them up and covered them with colored plastic electrician's tape, creating artistic designs. Then he let the air out and pulled the ball out from inside the tape leaving an interesting creation. He also liked to throw balls into the trees in the yard. The balls had to be perfect – at least what he considered perfect. If they were not to his specifications, he deemed them "rejects" and would have nothing to do with them. Shopping with him for perfect balls was an exercise in patience.

But we were all making progress.

The juggling act at home was fit for Barnum & Bailey. When I had an early morning meeting at St. Andrew's, Betsy got Jay on his bus before she went off to school. But on one particular day my car was being fixed, and a trustee from the school picked me up. He pulled into my driveway just as Jay managed to get to the very top of the pine tree in the yard. This elegant elderly man, dressed in a spotless suit, along with me, Betsy, Allison and Lulu the bus driver, coaxed Jay down. When we got into his car to go to our meeting, he said, "Mary, I don't know how you do it."

I thought, "You don't know the half of it. And you don't know how much better we're doing." I chuckled at the thought of this disparate little group at the mercy of a thirteen-year-old autistic boy sitting at the top of a pine tree.

L E S S O N 22

In the darkest of times, find the positive.
Look deep within yourself.

Chapter 23

A Time to Grow

After about a year at BDC, Jay entered the extended day program, staying at school until dinner time. This gave him a full day of academics and therapies, with an afterschool program focused on social interaction, conversation and play. How lucky he was. How lucky I felt.

His days were filled with activities with other children, including weekly outings aimed at developing social awareness. During lunches at local restaurants, staff members taught appropriate table manners while encouraging conversation. During mealtimes at home, he'll still say, "I am enjoying my dinner, Mummy," an appropriate observation, but also a mechanical throwback to his early days learning table behavior.

The teacher in me worried that his academic program wasn't strong enough, especially in reading. He was mastering a vocabulary of useful words, but didn't grasp the concept of reading for information or enjoyment. Since he couldn't think in the abstract, reading for fun was never going to be. I needed to put my own goals for him in perspective, acknowledging that the social skills he was acquiring were invaluable.

Jay also participated in a relaxation therapy program pioneered by the Grodens. At first he could follow the routine only with cues from a teacher or therapist, but eventually he began to use the tool spontaneously. Sitting on a chair with his hands in his lap, he recites, "Take a deep breath. Relax your head; relax your neck; relax your chest," and so on right down his body.

Jay still finds relaxation therapy a helpful stress-reducer, and will offer it to others if he perceives a need. Years ago Allison had a friend over who was in the midst of a teenage crisis. "Karen," he said, "you need to relax." He sat her in a chair and took her through the whole routine.

In the car when I sometimes swear at a careless driver, he often says, "Mummy, you are uptight. Take a deep breath and relax." Depending upon where we are, he goes through all or part of the procedure, often followed by, "Oh shoot, shoot, shoot is right, right, right," reminding me to clean up my language.

I wish I could have solved my own emotional issues as effectively as Jay solved his. About a year after Frank and I separated, he was fired. Though a little piece of me thought, "It serves him right," in reality he had been helping me pay the mortgage. I couldn't do it on my salary alone and would have to sell the house.

I expressed my fear and worry during a group therapy session. The therapist suggested I call Myrna, a realtor in Barrington. The session ended with a sendoff of good-lucks and high-fives.

Myrna turned out to be a terrific realtor, as well as a good friend, and sold my house in the fall of 1983, two years after we moved in. In a way it was a relief to leave a place permeated with so many painful memories. I found a nice little house to rent in the same neighborhood. It was on the market, but it was perfect for us, so I took a chance and rented it without a lease. Not a good decision. It sold in less than a year, and we had to move again.

This time I hit a roadblock. I couldn't find another place to rent in Barrington that would meet our needs. I looked at one house on the edge of town that was filthy – deep down dirty and smelly. I asked the owner if he would have it professionally cleaned, as it would require special equipment. He refused. I had only weeks to get out of my current rental and was beginning to panic.

At Lila's one evening, I sat in her family room sobbing, terrified of not having a place for me and my children to live, feeling like one of those "poor souls" she and I had sworn we'd never become. To my incredible relief, later that week I found a house that fit the bill. Feeling like a vagabond, I packed up and moved us to a three-bedroom Cape on a quiet street on the other side of town. This time I signed a lease.

The kids took the moves in stride. Even Jay rolled with the punches, each time settling in his own bedroom with all his familiar things. He also began to spend many weekends with his father and Hedi. When Betsy went off to college, Allison and I became a team at home.

But Allison's grades continued to slip. She failed two subjects her freshman year and had to make them up in summer school. To her horror, I took her out of public school and enrolled her at St. Andrew's. It had become coed the year before, with a program catering to underachievers. In one remarkable year, with the help of excellent teachers, she turned herself around. She rejoined her friends for her last two years, back in public school where she earned good grades. She was accepted at the college of her choice.

At thirteen, Jay became a Rhode Island Special Olympian. BDC encouraged the kids to participate in this terrific sporting event every spring at the University of Rhode Island. Weighing in at seventy-five pounds and standing four feet eight inches tall, he became a shot-putter, of all things, but he had excellent form. He "ran" track – looking like a stork – and participated in swimming events as well.

All of the Special Olympians stayed in the URI dorms and ate in the college dining hall. Family and friends came to cheer Jay on.

"How did you like your first Olympics, Jay?" I asked when he got home.

"It was a fun adventure," he replied.

"What was your favorite part of the weekend?"

"Eating hamburgers and French fries."

For the next fourteen years, Jay donned the blue and white uniform of BDC and collected a cache of ribbons to hang in his room.

While Frank and I were living separate lives, traveling parallel paths, the lines began to converge around Jay. We were able to talk about him and his needs, and it appeared Frank had chosen a partner who cared very much about our son. Jay looked forward to weekend visits with his dad, leaving me relieved to have the help, but hurting deeply over the new family structure unfolding.

As I watched the male component of my family drive away on Friday afternoons, sadness crept back into my heart. But I had no choice. I turned to my practical side and powered through it. These weekends gave me time for long runs with friends and time with my girls – for all of us, a time to grow.

In June, two years after our move to Rhode Island, our wonderful babysitter Sally drowned while swimming with friends in a quarry in Vermont. She was only twenty-one years old. Since Betsy and Allison were too young to remember when their Mimi died, this was my children's first encounter with death. It hit the girls very hard. Sally was part of our family. She spent many summers with us at the Cape, and we all felt the loss deeply.

Death is a difficult subject to discuss with any child. Jay was no exception. Leaving Jay at home with a sitter, Frank and I drove to the funeral together with Betsy and Allison, offering as much emotional support as we could. We talked about how fragile life is, how important it is to be conscious of safety, even though sometimes terrible accidents happen.

When we returned I asked Jay, "Do you know what happened to Sally?"

Showing no emotion, he answered, "Yes I do. Sally did die."

In Maryland years before Sally's death, Frank had given Jay a good wallop on his bottom for throwing a tube through a window. Jay responded, "Want to kill Daddy all dead." It was the first time I'd heard him use the word "dead," and I wondered if he knew what it meant.

In November of the year we lost Sally, my dad died of a massive stroke at the age of 85. Again the children were faced with death, and again Jay had no emotional response. But in the weeks that followed, he began to talk about dying, statements reflecting his fear. "I am healthy, Mummy. Daddy is not sick. I will not die."

I constantly assured him he was safe and healthy, as were the others in his family, but death remained an abiding fear in Jay for many years.

By fifteen, he was five feet tall and skinny, though a good eater. A late bloomer like his father, he hadn't begun to mature. In the next two years Jay grew six inches and gained twenty-eight pounds. With braces on his teeth, he was becoming a handsome teenager.

One evening when Jay was almost sixteen, he was lounging in the bathtub, still one of his favorite spots, when I heard a shriek from Allison. I bounded out of the kitchen fearing disaster. "What is it, Allie? What happened?"

"Mom," she exclaimed, "Jay has a pubic hair!"

We both laughed. "It's about time!" I declared.

He was indeed growing . . . maturing emotionally and physically. With that maturation, new issues and challenges awaited.

LESSON 23

Even if you are estranged from your spouse or partner, work together toward goals for your child.

Chapter 24

A Young Man Emerges

Hi, Mom," Betsy called as she came in the back door with friends. I was upstairs. Jay, I thought, was in his room.

"Oh, God!" Betsy shouted.

I dashed downstairs to find Jay on the floor, fully clothed, prone on a plastic shower curtain, his hands beneath him humping ferociously.

"Jay," I said, "please stand up." I took his hand and walked him to his room. "You do this only in private."

Betsy and her friends were more amused than shocked. One friend said, "It's just Jay being Jay." They had been watching Jay grow for years, and this was just another unusual behavior. But I felt embarrassed for Jay.

Autism doesn't preclude the development of sexual urges. However skewed the cognitive and emotional growth might be, physical development stays on a fairly traditional course.

Jay didn't like to be touched, nor did he show any attraction to girls or young women. For him sex had nothing to do with another person. As he explained, his short-lived period of touching breasts was because "I do like cones." But plastic was an obsession, so masturbation was usually accompanied by a plastic shower curtain.

In <u>Rainman,</u> Dustin Hoffman's character, Raymond, an autistic savant, walked in on his brother making love to his girlfriend, Susanna. Raymond simply sat on the end of the bed and turned on the television, oblivious. Later in the elevator, Susanna planted a kiss on Raymond's mouth and asked, "How was that?"

"That was wet," he replied with complete disinterest.

Jay displayed that same detachment from all things sexual.

The staff at BDC had developed a sex education curriculum, and I turned to them for help. BDC had been renamed The Groden Center in 1986, after the couple who founded it. The original name was too similar to that of a nearby school for autistic children that used Draconian means of discipline, including electric shock. In contrast, the Groden Center offered services in a compassionate environment sensitive to the needs of each person.

The sex education curriculum was divided into four levels. The first dealt with basic concepts of public vs. private, appropriate vs. inappropriate, strangers vs. friends, as well as hygiene and self-care. I met with Jay's teachers and we decided level one would be best for him.

Jay was processing both physical and emotional stimuli in a manner unique to him. He allowed me to hug him gently but was reluctant to let anyone else get that close. Sometimes people greeted him with a friendly pat on the back – not a welcome gesture – and when someone shook his hand he cautioned, "Please shake gently."

Certain sights and sounds were too much for Jay to process. The soft shutting of our screen door bothered him more than the loud slam of the car door. Some days he rode in the car with his eyes closed, complaining, "The sun is too bright," while on other days he stared right into the sun with no reaction. Bumps in the road caused by potholes drove him crazy.

Gradually he developed coping mechanisms. He used earplugs when he knew sounds would upset him, and he learned to use words to tell people they were too close. Bumps in the road remained problematic, although he could usually come to terms with them. "I do not like the bumps," he'd say. "I am going to call the governor."

Jay was a careful observer, keenly tuned in to sights, sounds and weather, reading the sky with amazing accuracy. "A storm is coming in from the west. It will snow," Jay would warn. He was rarely wrong. One day he observed, "Mummy, you cannot see the wind."

Awareness of his world extended to the stars and the planets. He began to identify the evening stars as they appeared. "There is Jupiter, Mummy."

I looked up at the sky and saw nothing. Jay knew exactly where Jupiter would be, and could identify its faint glow long before my eyes could find it

As Jay absorbed his world, learning to make it more comfortable, positive changes emerged in mine. One winter day in 1986, my realtor and good friend, Myrna, invited me to dinner. "We've invited our good friend, George Miller, and would love for you to meet him." When Myrna greeted me at the door that night, I looked straight through the foyer into the living room. A blazing fire cast a soft glow throughout the room, and a handsome man in a light gray suit stood next to the fireplace. His face lit up into a beautiful smile. I was smitten.

We started slowly, but by late spring we were a couple. By midsummer we had professed our love for each other on a Cape Cod beach.

George had lived in Barrington for many years before separating from his wife. He had two children, Susan and Chip, a friend of Betsy's. We liked each other's children, and two of them already were friends.

Jay, however, was a challenge for George. With all my insecurities about dating, I never saw my kids as a liability. I was incredibly proud of them and saw them as beautiful assets. I should have been more astute.

I thought back to the second or third date with a lawyer who arrived in his new Jaguar to meet Jay. He simply watched without comment. When he left, he found my cat, who had crawled into his car through the sunroof, meowing in the backseat. That was the end of that.

One date had to help get Jay down from a tree and another had to deal with a masturbating scene. I saw these incidents as comical. These men weren't important in my life, but George was different.

George liked Jay. Most everyone did, but while Jay was sweet-natured, he was also noisy with his EEEEEE sound and hand flapping. He still couldn't be left alone for any length of time. While George treated Jay with extreme kindness, he struggled with the intrusiveness.

For years George had been on the board of a well-known school for the physically handicapped in Rhode Island. He had served as chair and had spearheaded significant capital campaigns on behalf of the school, becoming an important spokesperson.

One day I asked him, not without trepidation, "How

can you be 'Mr. Wonderful' to this school, have your picture taken and appear on TV with handicapped children, but not be able to deal with a similar problem in your personal life?" I saw it as disingenuous, and I said so.

Incredibly, this beautiful man agreed. "Be patient with me, Mary. I love you, and I love your family."

In time, George developed a loving relationship with Jay, filled with humor and tenderness. He referred to Jay's shower curtain as his "Saturday night date" and treated him with sincere love and respect, joining my constant pursuit of a good life for my son.

After more than five years at St. Andrew's School, I was hired as Director of Development at Brown University's Medical School. As an alumnus of Brown, George was thrilled with my decision. The job required considerable travel, but Frank and Hedi were always willing to have Jay when I was gone.

Jay, too, had entered the job market, first as a volunteer at the South Providence Food Bank when he was sixteen. After a year there, he started part-time at Filene's Basement, along with two other Groden Center clients and a job coach.

"What do you do at Filene's Basement?" my friends often asked Jay.

"I do strip and hang," Jay replied, bringing the questioner up short.

Jay worked in the stockroom opening boxes of incoming inventory, stripping the plastic bags from the garments and hanging them on metal racks. At first I wondered if the plastic was a turn-on, but Jay said it was a "reject."

He loved his job "because I make moola, and I go to Pizzeria Uno for lunch." He sometimes added, "I do not like the noise the hangers make, but I am brave."

Acknowledging that he was brave was another coping mechanism. It carried over to all sorts of physical discomforts – bumping his elbow, skinning his knee, going to the dentist.

Over the years I had marched so steadily to a cadence of concern that when a new rhythm slipped into my life, it took me by surprise. Life was getting easier. Time seemed to speed by as Jay got older. He was becoming responsive and independent at home. I began to leave him alone for an hour or so to do an errand or to go out for a bite with George. Sometimes Jay even chose to go with us.

But autism doesn't have an age limit. It doesn't end when we eliminate the word "infantile." While there are reports of children being "cured," even those children carry some indication of autism for life.

Many of Jay's symptoms were being modified, and his growth and development were positive. But as he approached twenty-one, it was clear he would still require special services. The Groden Center was limited to children and young people under twenty-two, when the school systems terminate funding. The thought that Jay's services might be snatched from him terrified me. I started to put the wheels in motion for adult placement.

George supported my efforts in every way. He listened to my concerns and made suggestions, making phone calls if he had a contact he thought might help. He had become a true partner in all aspects of my life.

In June 1989, we were married on the deck of the townhouse we had bought in Bristol, Rhode Island, overlooking Narragansett Bay, before our families and the couple who introduced us. The weather was threatening, and Jay, looking handsome in his jacket and tie, kept track of it for us.

As we gathered outside to begin the ceremony, thunder rumbled in the distance, and George asked Jay, "When do you think the rain will start?"

"In twenty minutes," he answered with conviction.

Twenty minutes later, as I turned to kiss my new husband, raindrops fell on the shoulders of his navy blue blazer.

LESSON 24

Here comes puberty! Handle it openly and honestly.

Chapter 25

"Twenty-Two"

For the developmentally disabled, turning twenty-two is a big deal. At that arbitrary age the funding provided under public law 94-142, now called the Individuals with Disabilities Education Act, abruptly ends, and with it any services that funding provides. An autistic person transitioning from adolescence to adulthood today faces the same issues Jay faced twenty-five years ago. I began preparation well before "D-day."

A myriad of challenges, including heath care, must be addressed. When children outgrow pediatricians, new doctors take over, and for a child with special needs, the transition can be daunting.

As long ago as the 1980s, the medical community became increasingly aware of the growing number of special needs children entering adulthood. At a 1989 conference, "Growing Up and Getting Medical Care," then Surgeon General C. Everett Koop first used the word "transition" to refer to special needs adolescents entering the adult health care system. Since then structured transition programs have been developed.

Yet Dr. Debra Lotstein, Assistant Professor of Pediatrics at U.C.L.A., who studies the transition in young people with chronic medical conditions, recently reported that ". . .

gaps in care occur for as many as two-thirds of these young adults." Even with all the internet resources we have today, an army of parents out there does not have access. And twenty-five years ago neither did I.

"I want to make sure Jay has a physician like you," I explained to Jay's pediatrician. I wasn't trying to make him feel good. I was expressing my need to communicate openly about my son's health. Jay couldn't do it on his own.

"How about your own doctor?" he asked.

"My doctor's an OB/GYN," I replied with a grin.

He referred me to a primary care physician who agreed to take care of both Jay and me. As a handicapped adult, Jay remained covered under my insurance, and the transition was relatively easy.

But we weren't so lucky with dental care. Jay had completed his regimen of orthodontics and needed a new dentist. My own dentist refused to accept him as a Medicaid patient. I said I would cover the difference between what Medicaid paid and his price. Still the answer was "no."

"No?" How could he turn his back? Silently enraged, I left the office. I would have changed dentists, but he was an insurance client and friend of George's, so I faced a moral dilemma. Reluctantly, but without pressure from George, I stayed with my dentist and sought out a dentist for Jay who would accept Medicaid.

The dental office a friend suggested was in a rundown strip mall. Entering at the parking lot level, Jay and I climbed a dimly-lit stairway into a dingy office, where several dentists were filing indigent patients through like they were on an assembly line. After Jay's exam, we hurried out, knowing we wouldn't be back, and I quickly got Jay onto my dental policy. What a tragic testimony to the care available to those with no choices.

When Jay turned twenty-one, I didn't worry about his first legal beer, or graduate school or a job. My concern was that within a year he would lose the entire living and learning community where he was thriving.

In Jay's late teens, other symptoms had crept into his character, including an increase in ritualistic and compulsive behavior. He was diagnosed with obsessive/compulsive disorder (OCD) at seventeen. He washed his hands until they bled. He wouldn't step through a door until he'd tapped the door frame and returned several times to tap again. He wouldn't sit in a chair until he had brushed the seat thoroughly to remove any dirt, real or imagined. These new compulsions didn't cripple Jay, but they did interfere with his ability to listen and focus.

The Groden Center helped to address Jay's OCD and provided an amazing atmosphere to expand his horizons. But it would be up to me to secure state funds to access appropriate adult services. Jay was not able to make friends on his own, and without some kind of social structure, he would become a solitary person. Again, after so many years, I needed to find a placement for Jay.

The education transition challenge reminded me of an elderly widow who lived across the street from us in Barrington with her fifty-six-year-old "retarded" son, Francis. With only his mother to care for him, Francis stood at the edge of his front lawn waving at passing cars, his only connection to the outside world. I often stopped and talked with him about the weather, or his lunch, or whatever else his tiny world held.

Not long after we moved into the neighborhood, Francis's mother died, leaving him with no one. Neighbors told me that he was thriving in a group home, that he'd become more outgoing and engaged. He was enjoying movies and restaurants with his new housemates, meeting people and seeing a bigger world. What a testament to the capacity to grow, even into middle age. Francis was lucky. He landed in a perfect setting.

I knew that Jay had barely scratched the surface of what he could learn and become. He needed a full-time day program, but not just a sheltered workshop. He needed a place with a sense of community, where he could go to his job at Filene's Basement, continue his academics and his speech and occupational therapies. I couldn't bear to think Jay would lose these crucial services.

The Groden Center had expanded into the Groden Network of Services, including an excellent day program for autistic adults. The COVE Center (Community Opportunities in Vocation and Education) would be a natural step for Jay, shifting emphasis from academics to individual life skills, socialization, job placement and vocational skills. But unlike the under-twenty-two programs mandated by federal law, there was no mandate for this resource, no guarantee.

I would have to look to the state of Rhode Island for help in meeting Jay's needs and was urged to start seeking adult funding well before he turned twenty-one. "Get him in the pipeline now," people warned. "Money is tight."

State budget cuts are an ever-present threat to facilities like the Groden Network and to the special needs population. When I met with the Director of MHRH (Mental Health Retardation and Hospitals) to discuss funding, he made a poignant observation.

Staring out his window at the newly-built maximum security prison, he said, "It just seems wrong that the convicted felons have air-conditioned rooms, color TVs and clean new living space, when we have to fight for the smallest things for our special needs adults. The felons are there because of their crimes. Ours are where they are through no fault of their own."

I've never forgotten those words, spoken out of such frustration and with such deep commitment to those with developmental disabilities. Procuring funding for Jay as an adult would take hard work, just as the search for services had many years before, when he was a child. But this time services were in place. I wanted him to be at the COVE Center. I just needed to access it.

I wrote to the governor's office and to other state offices advocating for Jay and others like him. I met many times with the Department of Developmental Disabilities and filled out endless forms. The psychiatrist who saw Jay on an annual basis wrote a strong letter substantiating the need for continued services.

The battle had begun, with big guns and small.

—

LESSON 25

Plan ahead. You have a powerful voice. Use it.

Chapter 26

The Bird Spreads His Wings

Happy birthday to you
Happy birthday to you. . .

On a December night in 1991, we all sang to Jay on his twenty-second birthday: George and I, his dad and Hedi and little sister, Emily, and a gang of special young people from a group Jay had just joined called "Stepping Out." We had a holiday grab bag for everyone and the guest of honor was ecstatic, opening a kaleidoscope, a huge orange gym ball, Toblerone candy bars, beach balls, and of course, clothes from Mom and Dad. With each gift Jay responded in his monotone, "Thank you. I do like this," but the sparkle in his eyes revealed what his tone could not.

Just weeks before, Jay's adult funding had come through. The hard work had paid off, and he had moved on to the COVE Center, a natural step and great opportunity. It was truly a time to celebrate: Jay's birthday, his acceptance and funding for COVE, and his new group of friends.

Stepping Out was an innovative program founded a few years earlier by a small group of parents who had young adults with developmental disabilities. Recognizing that their adult children had no avenues for social interaction beyond school and work, they organized about twenty young people to meet for weekend social events.

Many members of Stepping Out lived at home. Some lived in group homes, and a couple lived independently. But each was isolated socially by his disability. None drove a car and none had a network of friends. Unlike other young people, none of them could call a friend to go to a movie, play ball or even hang out at the mall, because each needed some level of supervision. This terrific program expanded the community where Jay and his friends lived and learned.

Pat, a young woman who had made her mark both as a teacher and administrator at COVE, directed and chaperoned the Stepping Out activities. COVE staff provided transportation to overnight camping trips, movies and dinners, dances and parties, museums, sporting events, zoos, and in the summer, cookouts and swim parties at members' family homes. Jay's birthday party became an annual Stepping Out event.

The program provided a unique opportunity for both the young people and their parents. At some point we sacrifice our own social lives for our children's, staying home to make sure kids are in on time, driving to play dates and hosting sleepovers. Most parents find more time for their own interests as their children reach maturity, but not so for the parents of special needs youngsters. Their maturity does not necessarily mean independence. Challenges and commitments for parents like me only intensify. Stepping Out offered great activities for our children and a welcome respite for many parents.

I became an active member of the governing board, eventually serving as president. Parents and staff met twice a year to discuss plans and manage finances. The group was supported by an annual membership fee, and our 501c3 tax status allowed us to receive tax deductible gifts. We submitted grant proposals to local foundations for additional program support.

George and I hosted many Stepping Out gatherings at our place in Bristol. Besides Jay's birthday parties, each summer for many years the group came out for a day, took rides in our boat, went swimming and played games. Eating was the favorite activity, so we always wrapped things up with a big cookout.

Jonathan, a young man with autism, was nervous about getting into the boat, a new experience for him. "No thank you, Mrs. Miller. I'll just watch."

I took his hand, coaxed him into a life jacket and onto the boat, and sat with him for a short ride. By the time we got back to the dock he was grinning from ear-to-ear and eager to go again.

I had great conversations with some of the other members. With Susan I talked about clothes, her passion, and with Christa about her plans for the International Special Olympics. John liked you to tell him your birthdate so he could calculate in seconds the day of the week you were born.

Many members were considerably higher functioning than Jay, and I worried at first. But time and again he rose to the occasion and astonished me with his ability to enjoy these friends in his own way. While he rarely initiated conversation, he was responsive and enthusiastically participated in the activities.

It was amazing, fun, exhilarating really, to watch the members of Stepping Out grow and expand their horizons, interacting with friends, laughing and goofing around just like any other group of young people, and it was Jay's introduction to a community larger than family and school.

At home Jay was occupied with his "projects," taping his plastic beach balls and making sculptures out of tubes and pieces of plastic. But other artistic instincts were also emerging. He loved to draw pictures of his favorite things: water towers, beach balls, lighthouses, and fill them in with unexpected colors, using magic markers to create impressionistic images.

Through the COVE Center, he began selling these pieces at the annual Thayer Street Art Festival in Providence. Many of my friends became "collectors" of Jay's work. He didn't give his artwork away, though. It had a price. He'd even do a "commissioned" work if a friend asked. He did a great stylized drawing of a martini glass for a martini-loving friend, and also drew a colorful version of Tigger, our cat.

Jay's whole family became fans of his artwork. He now had two stepparents who embraced his talents and interests, and accepted him into their lives with love and respect. I initially struggled with this dynamic, and in the early years kept a respectful distance from Jay's dad and stepmother. But the distance was bridged gradually by good communication regarding our son and his needs.

George played a central role. He possessed a deep sense of decency and got along with Frank, encouraging me to do what I felt was right. As a team we became a strong positive force in Jay's life, as parents and advocates.

Jay was nineteen when his baby sister was born to Frank and Hedi. His gentle nature was reflected in the way he treated her, giving her soft pats and tender kisses on her forehead, repeating, "I do love my sister, Emily. I am a good big brother."

Jay's world was expanding. To grow emotionally and socially, he needed more independence. He needed to "step out" further into the world, learning new life skills and gaining a greater sense of self-reliance. At home I tended to spoil him, doing his laundry, making his bed, cooking his meals. Away from home, he would have to learn to do for himself.

While pursuing placement in an adult day program, I began to explore future residential options, looking for a place where Jay would have the chance to extend his independence, to learn living skills.

First I needed to know he would be safe, surrounded by responsible, trustworthy people. Stories of mistreatment and abuse of our special needs population flow through some institutions like polluted water. While reading a newspaper exposé about the unconscionable mistreatment of developmentally disabled patients in a state-run institution in the northeast, I had to put the paper down after the first few paragraphs, unable to read on. It took me time to get through the account of "beating retards" with a "magic wand" kept hidden in a desk drawer, and the death of a thirteen-year-old autistic boy who was suffocated by his "caregivers."

Jay was still so vulnerable. He knew only to trust. He accepted the spoken word at face value, unable to read facial expressions. Finding a place where he would be treated with dignity and respect was essential.

Everyone firmly believed a move would be a positive step for Jay. Staff members at COVE encouraged me to "get the wheels in motion," as it could be a long process. The same psychiatrist who supported Jay's need for adult day services emphasized in a follow-up report the benefits a twenty-four-hour program would offer.

Jay did not share my enthusiasm in the least. "It is just a suggestion, Mummy," he'd say, his favorite reply when he didn't agree with me.

"Jay," I explained, "Betsy and Allison went away to college when they were eighteen and now have apartments of their own. You will be doing the same thing."

He didn't buy it. Who could blame him? It was a scary concept, and he had a great setup at home. We loved having Jay with us and explained that if he ever moved to his own place, he would always have his room with us. I also assured him that it had to be his decision.

It was a scary idea for me too, though I knew it was an important next step. I studied the Groden Network's excellent organization of group homes and other living options.

One possibility was the Professional Family Living Arrangement (PFLA), a creative plan that provided a living situation for one special needs adult in the home of a Groden Network professional. A less dramatic move than a group home, it still provided a level of independence from family. Funding was also more readily available, as it was less expensive. I felt most comfortable with this choice, but our boy still wasn't buying.

Jay's Stepping Out staff leader was interested in having Jay come to live with her and her family as part of the PFLA program. Jay knew Pat, and more importantly, *I* knew her. I had watched her in action with the Stepping Out group. She and her soon-to-be husband owned a house where they lived with Pat's two daughters. Pat invited George, Jay and me to a cookout to meet the family. We toured the house, looked at what would be Jay's room and enjoyed a delicious supper on the front porch. It was a nice spot on a quiet street near the village center.

"Jay, would you like to come here to live with us?" Pat asked.

"No thank you, Pat. I will stay at my mom's and my dad's house."

"Well, Jay, would you like to come for a sleep-over? We could do something fun like go to the mall, and you could just try out the room."

Jay agreed, and a date was set. Both Jay and Pat reported a nice evening, though in the middle of the night Pat was awakened by Jay pulling on her pillow.

"Jay, what are you doing?" asked a startled Pat.

A matter-of-fact Jay answered, "I do need another pillow for my head."

The next morning he stayed in the shower for twenty minutes and then used three towels to dry off.

They had a lot to learn about each other, so Pat and her family planned other evenings with Jay. I, too, needed reassurance that this was the best move. Without exception the visits were successful, and Jay finally agreed to give the new living arrangement a try.

Moving day was a momentous occasion. Jay and I had bought a new comforter and sheets for his bed, and he picked out a rug and curtains. With a packed car, we first stopped at McDonalds for his favorite lunch: a hamburger, French fries and a Coke. On the way to Pat's we talked about how grown up he was becoming and how proud we were of him.

"I am proud of myself," he responded. What a milestone!

Jay formed a warm bond with his new housemates, Pat and John, who were not much older than he was. Even Pat's daughters welcomed Jay into their house. The thirteen-year-old often walked with Jay to get ice cream in the village where everyone was getting to know him.

The setup worked well, but the transition wasn't without incidents. Early on, Pat felt Jay was responsible enough to learn to take public transportation. With input from other staff at COVE and with my blessing, she arranged for Jay to take the Rhode Island Public Transportation Authority bus from his new home to COVE, several towns away, a trip that involved changing buses in Providence. After many runs with Pat and others, the staff decided he was ready to make the trip alone.

While I was out of town on business, Jay's dad received a phone call from the East Providence Police Station. The police had Jay in custody! He had needed to go to the bathroom, and asking for a men's room had not been part of his training, so he urinated in public. But he had his ID card and knew the important phone numbers.

My heart stopped when I imagined him in the police station alone. I was unsure of my footing as I sought the fine line between independence and safety for Jay.

Pat and I were able to talk through the incident, analyzing what went wrong and how to move forward. Stopping independent bus travel for a while, we concentrated on learning life skills closer to home.

With a deep belief in Jay, Pat became a pivotal force in his life, guiding him toward independence. She made more demands on him than I, sometimes to Jay's irritation. But we were able to address issues as they arose, including the OCD, which was beginning to interfere more and more with his ability to function effectively.

L ESSON 26

Take chances!

Chapter 27

Challenges

Jay was compulsively clean. His hand-washing routine became a source of concern, especially in the winter when his hands chafed and bled. After his shower, if the exact pair of underwear was not right within his reach, he became immobilized, saying, "I am stranded." After a bowel movement, he used reams of toilet paper, spending an inordinate amount of time in the bathroom.

A new psychiatrist prescribed Anafranil, an antidepressant used successfully to ameliorate OCD behaviors. Jay started the medicine a few months after moving in with Pat and John, and the results were good. But I noticed from time to time Jay had an upset stomach. He also began to lose a little weight. At five feet nine and only one-hundred-twenty pounds, he couldn't afford to lose an ounce. His doctor couldn't find a reason for the upsets, and neither of us connected the Anafranil to the problem.

On a May afternoon in 1993, George picked Jay up for Allison's wedding weekend. George had just bought a brand new car the day before.

"I do like your new car, George," Jay commented as he climbed into the backseat where he always chose to ride. He hummed and rocked, excited about the celebration ahead.

But shortly before they got home, Jay got violently sick. George cleaned Jay up as best he could with his handkerchief and hurried home to finish the job. He then calmly hosed out the new car, focusing his concern on Jay.

Jay was fine that evening at the rehearsal dinner, and the next day at church, handsome in a black tuxedo, he walked me down the aisle. He danced with his sisters, the bride and maid of honor, and enjoyed a wedding feast, cake and all.

With the wedding excitement, we forgot the vomiting incident. But several weeks later the COVE Center called to say Jay had vomited to the point of dehydration, and had been taken to a local emergency room. Having covered all the bases with his doctor, I realized that the medication must be causing the nausea. Jay's doctor decided to wean him off the Anafranil, and the vomiting episodes stopped.

But Jay's weight loss frightened me. He had dropped to one-hundred-fifteen pounds, and his face bones stuck out. Pat and our family got on the "weight-gain bandwagon," monitoring his meals and encouraging him to eat more heartily. He had always been motivated by "moola," so I offered thirty dollars if he got his weight up to one-hundred-thirty. His new psychiatrist saw him every couple of months, to monitor his weight and guide him through a new drug protocol for OCD. He got his weight up to one-hundred-thirty – with his shoes on – and earned the thirty dollars.

Jay still needed help with his OCD. Despite daily behavior therapy, the obsessive/compulsive rituals had a firm grip on his life. His psychiatrist prescribed Prozac, which helped without any apparent side effects. He was less anxious, able to control the door tapping and hand washing, and his weight stayed consistent at about one-hundred-thirty.

A year and a half after Allison's wedding we brought Jay to the Cape for Betsy's turn at the altar. At the rehearsal dinner the bride and groom gave gifts to members of the wedding party. Jay's box contained a wad of one dollar bills – one-hundred to be exact. Ecstatic, he jumped to his feet, exclaiming, "Look at all the moola for me!" He got a great round of applause.

Jay did beautifully at the large Catholic wedding, watching the other groomsmen, following them to the altar for Communion. Knowing Jay was not a Catholic, one of the other groomsmen gently guided him back to watch. On the rare occasions when Jay attended church with Pat or me, and the minister started to pray, Jay closed his eyes, crossed his fingers, arms and legs and whispered, "I am praying for good weather." Whatever higher power he invokes, his prayers are concrete.

Jay also abides by a literal code that helps him decipher the difference between right and wrong. One day out of the blue he firmly announced, "Ain't is a bad word."

"Who told you that?" I replied.

He said someone at COVE used the word, and was told it was a bad word. I tried to explain to him that it wasn't proper English, but it wasn't a bad word.

"Is it a swear?" he asked, ever watchful about the use of such language.

Again I attempted to clarify the difference between the use of a swear word and the use of an incorrect word such as ain't, but to no avail. If it's a bad word, it must be a swear. If it's not a swear, why is it a bad word? Around and around we went. Jay sometimes gets lost in the subtleties.

Less than two years after Jay moved in with Pat, she gave

birth to a baby girl. Jay welcomed Jillian as he had his own baby sister, but the house was small and he found her crying difficult to tolerate.

With Pat, we decided to look for another living arrangement. Feeling Jay was ready, we found space at one of the Groden group homes. It turned out to be a nightmare. The other clients were noisy, generally lower functioning, and Jay complained that the home in northern Rhode Island was too far from his family. After months of searching, we found an apartment in Providence for Jay to share with another young man and a full-time staff person provided through the Groden Center.

Another bad move. We never found an appropriate apartment mate, and Jay was very lonely. He grew quiet and constantly asked to come home for visits. He didn't act out, but he wasn't his enthusiastic self, counting water towers from the car or gleefully throwing plastic balls into trees. He had lost his sense of community.

Again, I was unsure about my decisions for Jay. But after these early stumbles, we found the perfect setup in an unexpected place – right back with Pat.

Jillian was no longer an infant, and Pat and John had purchased a larger house with a basement apartment. With his own bedroom and bathroom, he was on cloud nine. He saw Pat, John and Jillian as part of his family, and the new house was much closer to us. He would live there for the next eleven years.

But as Jay was settling into his new digs, Filene's Basement closed, leaving him out of a job he loved, where he had accepted yearly employment pins with great pride. He tried working at a college campus recycling center, but hated it because it was dirty. He did odd jobs at COVE, in the laundry and the office, but the Filene's void remained.

Searching diligently, COVE's job coordinator found the perfect spot for Jay at Domino's Pizza, folding boxes. The work was precise, repetitive and clean. He loved it. He counted the boxes he folded, and at 500,000, a staff member suggested he should be in the Guinness Book of World Records! Jay still goes to Domino's three days a week and has folded more boxes than even he can count.

With a new job and a terrific living setup, Jay's world continued to evolve. His OCD seemed to be under control. He had dealt with birth, death, job changes and moves, and Stepping Out was broadening his social experiences. One spring Saturday the group went all the way to the Bronx Zoo. Jay loved the trip and started to talk about traveling.

Early in 1991, he took his first airplane trip with his stepmother and sister, Emily. "I did see a view," he reported. It was no longer pronounced the "biew" he saw from the tallest tree in our yard.

"I would like to take a trip with my mom," Jay said after his return.

The seed was planted for the traveling twosome.

L E S S O N 27

Don't allow your child to become isolated.
Create a community.

Chapter 28

A Traveling Man

We're off to see the wizard, the Wonderful Wizard of Oz . . ." Jay's deep monotone echoed down the jetway leading to the plane. Passengers turned to look, some startled, even a little fearful, but most smiling. Jay couldn't contain his excitement at the prospect of our flight to Orlando.

I wouldn't have attempted such a trip when Jay was younger, but his ability to wait patiently in restaurants and supermarkets had developed over the years. Our family automobile trips had been great adventures from the time he was a small boy. He rocked merrily in the backseat carefully watching the world pass by. He was now eager for greater adventures.

The plane lifted off into a sunny April sky, and Jay tracked our progress from the window seat. "I see New York City," he exclaimed, his instinctive sense of direction amazing me. "We are over New Jersey. That is Maryland down there now."

When we were over states he'd never been in, he wanted to know where they were – south of Virginia, next to the ocean – and what they were called.

"Would you like to look at a map when we get to Florida?" I asked.

"No thank you," he replied. He already had the map in his head.

Landing in Orlando, we rented a car and drove to our hotel at Disney. The trip through Magic Kingdom later that day, seen through the eyes of a young man with autism, was untraditional. No scary "Space Mountain" for him! Instead, after gentle sails through "It's a Small World" and "Pirates of the Caribbean," Jay slipped through the crowds, seeking out every pole, hydrant and post, any cylinder he could find. Stopping from time to time for a closer look, he put his fingers in front of his eyes like a surveyor taking a measurement. Then, flapping his hands excitedly, he again sprinted forward.

It was a joyful, high-energy tour of the park, topped off with a visit to a gift shop where he chose Disney figurines and blow-up beach balls. My boy sure loved to shop.

For the first time, I needed to let Jay go into the men's room alone. "Jay," I warned, "you know not to talk to anyone you don't know or let anyone touch you."

"Yes I do, Mummy," he replied as he dashed into the dark shadows of the men's room.

I waited nervously outside the door, feeling like a loitering weirdo. Too much time was passing. I called out, "Jay, please hurry." No response.

Out of desperation, I asked a young man going in if he would check on my son. I described Jay, and the young man was willing and understanding, kind really. Jay emerged, hands and face soaked.

"You can't spend that much time in restrooms," I told him. "That worries me. You have to wash your hands more quickly."

Jay furrowed his brow, looking grave. "You don't want to lose me," he replied, recognizing the intensity of my emotions.

"You're right, Jay. I love you very much."

"I do love you too, Mummy."

Such acts of kindness would be repeated often during our travels over the years. People were usually nice to Jay, engaging him in conversation. "What's your name? Where are you going? Are you having fun?" These simple questions elicited eager answers and broad, toothy grins.

Occasionally fear entered the equation. Hearing Jay's deep staccato voice or watching his odd movements, some scurried away, especially mothers with young children. Understanding their fear, I still felt burned. I wanted to talk to them, but didn't know what to say. Instead, I smiled, engaging Jay in normal conversation to show he was a gentle young man.

The Americans with Disabilities Act, implemented in 1990, one year before our first trip, initiated huge changes in the lives of those with disabilities and in the general public's attitude toward them. Hotels and resorts began to welcome guests with special needs. Some had designated dining rooms where trained professionals supervised special needs children, allowing parents time for a quiet dinner. How dramatically attitudes have changed since Jay was only two, and we were asked to leave a Howard Johnson's restaurant because of the noises he made.

The next day we had a ringside seat at Sea World before heading to Naples to visit Barrie and her husband. With Jay rocking in the backseat to his favorite tunes, we drove down Route 27, a two-lane road along the spine of Florida. Passing through tiny towns surrounded by miles of orange groves, we talked about the warm climate being perfect for growing oranges and grapefruit, fruit he loved. "Florida is near the equator. The sun is closer," Jay instinctively observed.

In a few hours we came to the proverbial fork in the road, and without consulting my map, I stayed on Route 27. A mile or two down the road Jay piped up, "Mummy, we are going in the wrong direction."

"No we're not, Jay," I replied with conviction. "We're heading to Naples on the west coast."

"This is the wrong direction, Mummy. The sun is back there." Jay pointed over his head to the rear window where the sun was streaming through.

Sure enough, after stopping to consult my map, I realized we were on the road to Palm Beach, heading due east. This wouldn't be the last time Jay would tell me I was going in the wrong direction.

In Naples that evening we went to the Sunset Bar, an outdoor restaurant on the beach, and watched the sun fall into the Gulf of Mexico. Jay was mesmerized, looking between his fingers until the red ball finally disappeared. The next day we took a boat tour, exploring the waterways around Naples where Jay was entertained by dolphins and flying fish.

When it was time to go home, Jay became agitated. He glared at me with his body tensed, a typical posture when he was anxious or distressed. After asking him a few questions, I realized he was upset about leaving. While a natural reaction for anyone having a good time, it was difficult to help Jay understand his own feelings. He was quiet all the way to the airport.

"I feel the same way about leaving, Jay, but we both have to get back to our jobs and our regular life in Rhode Island."

I'd been recruited away from the medical school that year to raise money for a teaching hospital in Providence. While my vacation package was generous, I still had to count days off, and I explained this to Jay. I also reminded him that the people at his workplace also depended on him.

Jay handled his agitation as he often did, by asking the same questions over and over. "Why does Mummy have to work? Why do I live in Rhode Island? Why is the water tower in East Providence?"

He wasn't looking for answers. The rhetorical and sometimes nonsensical questions were a release, a way for him to process the situation. By the time we got on the plane he had calmed down, but he reacted this way at the end of every trip for the next couple of years.

As soon as we returned from Florida, Jay decided that trip was only the beginning of his travels. Betsy had taken a marketing job outside of Los Angeles, and we decided to visit her. She shared a two-bedroom apartment with a young woman who went to stay with a friend, giving us her bedroom for the long weekend.

Around this time, Jay developed another obsession. He didn't like ragged edges on things such as rugs, pictures or paper, and used scissors to smooth the corners, once cutting away a large part of a favorite Oriental rug before I realized what he was doing. While visiting Betsy, Jay cut the edges on a pile of photos on her apartment mate's dresser.

"Why did you do this, Jay?" I asked.

"Because I do want the edges to be smooth."

"But these aren't your pictures. If you do things like this when we visit people, we won't be able to take any more trips together."

When we returned home, Jay looked for reassurance that we would be able to travel again. He said he wanted to visit our old neighborhood in Maryland and Washington DC. While assuring him that would be possible, I didn't let him forget the photo incident.

A year later, we took the first of three trips to Maryland and spent a day in Washington. Our visit to the Air and Space Museum was reminiscent of Disney, intense and exhausting, covering every inch of the museum. I was relieved when he agreed to sit and watch the IMAX movie.

We didn't sit for long. A trip up the Washington Monument was at the top of his list, and in spite of an hour-long wait, he insisted. Though not quite a cylinder, the monument's shape fascinated Jay. As soon as we left the elevator at the top, he exclaimed, "What a view!" Identifying the Capitol and pointing in the direction of our old house in Maryland, Jay established his own place in the universe.

Having learned a lesson from our earlier departures, this time we talked about the number of days we'd be gone and exactly when we'd return. It worked. When it was time to leave, he simply sat back and enjoyed the ride home.

Jay was becoming an old hand at travel. He reveled in seeing new places, and the scope of his world expanded with visits to destinations nationwide. In a way, these trips were a measuring stick for his growth. Restrooms were no longer an issue. He became more conversant, developing a love for restaurant dinners. My copilot no longer prefers the backseat, but sits in the front with me, manning the radio and keeping an ever-vigilant eye on our path.

In 1996 we tried a "three-day fun-filled Carnival Cruise" to the Bahamas. Fun-filled for whom I wasn't sure. But Jay was excited about going outside of the United States on a big ship. He loved his dad's boat and our little outboard on Narragansett Bay in Rhode Island.

The huge Carnival Cruise ship was an entirely different experience. The ship's lobby was several stories high. Jay stopped dead in his tracks. "Whoa, this is fancy!" he exclaimed.

Gaudy might have been a better word, but Jay was entranced.

The next day we took an excursion to "The Blue Lagoon," on a small island owned by the cruise line. Jay had his disposable underwater camera with him, but refused to use it in the water.

"Why won't you use your camera?" I asked.

"I do want to save it for later."

"Later" turned out to be a wade in the eighteen-inch kiddies' pool on the ship, where he took pictures of underwater, cylindrical pipes.

One evening during dinner, Jay remarked, "Mummy, it does feel like morning."

"Why is that, Jay?"

"Because the sun is over there; the ship is going in a different direction."

My boy was right again. Someone on board had gotten sick, and the ship had turned 180 degrees to take that person to a nearby island. The shift made Jay feel like it was sunrise instead of sunset. With an elemental connection to the world and an awareness of place lost on others, he had a unique insight into our journey.

I loved traveling with Jay (he insisted no one else travel with us), but if I sought out destinations to visit friends and relatives, it was easier for me and generally more fun.

In 1999 we took the first of three trips to visit my brother in Mesquite, Nevada, seventy-five miles north of Las Vegas. Hikes in the magnificent canyons of southern Utah were thrilling, and standing atop the Hoover Dam, Jay was captivated by yet another amazing view. Taking in the sights and lights of Las Vegas, my unerring pathfinder navigated The Strip.

Jay also became a proficient and independent bus traveler. That same year, 1999, George and I sold our place in Bristol and bought a small condo in Providence, Rhode Island. We also bought a weekend house in Chatham on Cape Cod, hoping to retire there one day. Jay loved coming to the Cape any time of year, taking the bus alone for visits.

By bus, car, boat or plane, he loved his trips. Frank's younger brother and his wife invited Jay and me to visit them in northern California in April 2004 where we stayed in a motel near their small house. Steve, a successful commercial fisherman, took us for a sunset cruise on Half Moon Bay aboard the Mr. Morgan, his huge commercial fishing vessel. Watching the sun slip below the rim of the Pacific Ocean, Jay became fascinated with the Pacific sky. Gathered around a bonfire on the beach that night after dinner, we roasted marshmallows while Jay identified stars floating above the Pacific.

"Tomorrow we will *walk* across the Golden Gate Bridge," Jay announced.

"Why don't we drive across?" I asked.

"Because my friend, John (Pat's husband) did say we could walk across."

We did indeed walk over and back, a mile-and-a-half each way, before driving to the Muir Woods, a forest of towering redwoods.

"Whoa, these are the biggest trees I have ever seen," Jay marveled.

The next day we drove to San Francisco for lunch at Fishermen's Wharf, and then to the airport hotel. Each trip seemed better than the one before.

LESSON 28

New environments reveal so much.
You learn while your child does.

Chapter 29

Bumps in the Road

As Jay moved into his mid-thirties, he continued to grow in so many positive ways, both at home and while traveling. Yet certain features of his OCD were again escalating, with outbursts bordering on the psychotic. Potholes in the road sent him into a frenzy. His explosions became more frequent and violent, more difficult for him and those around him. Erupting several times in the COVE Center van, he tried to kick out the windows.

When I hit one of the dreaded potholes, Jay flew into a rage, his voice a bullhorn emitting a loud, desperate wail. When I tried to settle him down, he began to sob, a visceral, throaty howl from deep within. Between sobs he shouted, "I hate the water tower in East Providence! I don't want to live with Pat! I hate the bumps!"

I was afraid, not of Jay, but of what was happening. In one instant, it seemed all the progress we'd made was reduced to a gargantuan psychotic episode. I calmed him down by talking about other things. But in the ensuing weeks the flare-ups continued, both at home and at COVE, with his anger at Pat increasing.

Was he really unhappy at Pat's? I knew Jay's environment was more structured there than at home, but he had always appeared happy. And when he was stressed, he always said he didn't like things I knew he liked, like the water tower in East Providence. Was something going on at COVE? Whatever it was, Jay was unable to express it. I knew I needed help, so I looked to a new resource.

In late 2000, I established a small consulting firm with a colleague I'd worked with both at Brown and at the hospital. One of our major contracts was a fundraising project for the psychiatric teaching hospital affiliated with Brown. There I met a psychiatrist who was an international pioneer in the treatment of OCD. Though he'd never treated a person with autism, he agreed to meet with Pat, Jay and me.

At our first meeting we talked about Jay's outbursts and his anger with Pat. Our conversation touched a nerve, and Jay broke into a fit of deep desperate sobs, exhibiting the very behavior which brought us there. "I don't want to live with Pat!" he shouted. "I don't want to go to COVE!"

We were able to talk him down, but he still couldn't express what was causing his anxiety. It was clear he needed help.

Jay was taking 40 milligrams of Prozac, and the doctor recommended changing the prescription to 40 milligrams of Celexa, another antidepressant, in addition to 25 milligrams of Risperdal, an antipsychotic drug. Ever reluctant to over-medicate Jay, I cautiously accepted the protocol. The new combination worked miracles, with no side effects. Jay became able to simply say, "I do not like the bumps." And his anger at Pat subsided.

After a couple of follow-up visits, we decided the change in medication was indeed the solution. For a long time I feared another episode, but none came. Fortunately, none of the outbursts had occurred while we were traveling.

At home Jay's gentle nature reemerged and was reflected in his treatment of his little nieces and nephew. As with his sister Emily, he treated Allison's daughters, Samantha and Katie, and Betsy's children Maddie, Caroline and William, with pats and airy kisses. As they grew, they in turn accepted Jay with great affection. He's always welcome when he comes to visit for a weekend or when he shows up for one of their lacrosse or basketball games.

Our annual excursions continued with ever-widening horizons. My brother had moved to central Mexico and was eager for us to visit. Jay was ecstatic about traveling to a different country, a plan that would require a passport. This was *really* traveling! While others stood impatiently in line for passport applications, Jay grinned from ear-to-ear for over an hour, taking deep relaxation breaths to contain his excitement.

The trip was a huge success. Jay practiced a few words of Spanish, getting a great kick out of "gracias" and waiting expectantly for the requisite "denada." As we bounced along the cobblestone streets in my brother's old pickup truck, Jay never said a word about the bumps.

On the unpaved, rutted streets of a nearby village, cows roamed freely, and more people rode on horseback than in cars. Never mentioning the bumps, Jay declared, "This is like the olden days," a concept of time I didn't know he possessed.

The next year Jay wanted to visit Steve and Mary again in Half Moon Bay, California. Every year as we looked forward to April, we discussed our plans: where we would go, what we would do. The anticipation was half the fun for both of us. This time we planned for the Aquarium in La Jolla and the boat trip to Alcatraz, as well as lunch at Fishermen's Wharf in San Francisco.

We had plane tickets and reservations at the same motel, but our trip would need to be postponed. This April would be different.

LESSON 29

Take on the bumps. You have a deeper well of solutions than you think.

Chapter 30

April

"April is the cruelest month," wrote T. S. Eliot. Palm Sunday fell in early April 2006, just days before our trip to California. The day was cloudy, with a cold wind blowing off the ocean in Chatham. Allison, Ray and their daughters, Samantha, ten, and Katie, seven, were visiting for the weekend. George and Katie went out for breakfast, their favorite morning routine, and later Ray, George and I bundled up to brave nippy golf at the local nine-hole course.

George and I were fairly new golfers, and though our scorekeeping was casual, we loved to compete. George hit a great drive off the seventh tee, high over a marsh and over the ladies' tee. As he walked by, I gave him a congratulatory kiss and told him I loved him, but I was up a stroke. He smiled, his eyes twinkling, and turned to hike up the steep hill to his ball on one side of the fairway, while I went to mine on the other.

Suddenly Ray shouted, "Mary, come quick!"

I looked, but didn't see George. Dropping my club, I dashed to the other side of the fairway to find him on the ground. My steadfast son-in-law immediately called 911 as I knelt to tend to my dearest George. His eyes were open. He lifted his knees to his chest and rolled on his side. Then he was still. "OK," I thought. "He's just passed out."

Cell phone still pressed to his ear, Ray turned George onto his back. Just one of his beautiful blue eyes stared. The other was closed. Coached by the 911 operator, we administered CPR while waiting for the ambulance.

Our location on the golf course was the farthest point from any road, so the medics had to climb the hill to reach us. "Hurry," I screamed, and they began to run. Kneeling, I closed George's other eye. So he could sleep.

As they worked on my husband, I turned away, pacing, worrying the love of my life into being OK. Lifting George gently onto a stretcher, they rushed him to the ambulance. "Is this really happening?" I thought, "or is it a dreadful nightmare?" I started to shiver as the medics carried my lifeless love away from me. I tried to climb into the ambulance, but they turned me away.

Allison had arrived at the golf course with her cousin, Jen, who drove me to Cape Cod Hospital in Hyannis to meet George. A staff person took us to the "family room," where I called Betsy and her husband. I also called George's children, Chip and Susan, in Rhode Island. Their father had collapsed on the golf course, I told them. They should get to the hospital as soon as possible.

The doctors worked on George for another hour. Finally, a young physician called me aside. "Your husband has never regained consciousness," he said, "and we have not been able to get a spontaneous heartbeat. We're sorry to tell you there is nothing more we can do. We recommend that treatment be stopped."

With all the calmness I didn't know I possessed, I gave the doctor permission to stop treatment and let him go.

Over the years, George and I had talked about the end of life. We didn't want heroics to preserve us as vegetables. But I never thought I'd be called to the task. I now found myself in yet another role. A widow.

Allison called Pat at home that Sunday afternoon, and Pat took Jay to the beach, where she told him about George's death. They walked and talked, and for the first time death brought Jay to tears. They stayed home from COVE the next day and planted a rosebush in the yard for George. It blooms every spring to this day.

My condo in Providence became command central. Chip and my friend Myrna came with me to the funeral home to make arrangements. As we were leaving, I realized I'd forgotten my glasses and returned to get them. Walking back to the car, I felt I was looking at myself from outside my body. I saw a tiny being, much smaller than life-sized, walking along the sidewalk from the funeral home, alone. My vulnerability terrified me.

But my family surrounded me. When Jay joined us all in Providence I opened my arms and gave him a big hug. "I am so so so sad that George did die," he said flatly. "I will take care of you, Mummy. I am healthy. We will still go on our trip."

There they were, all of Jay's sweet sentiments wrapped into a few words: sadness for George, concern for me and for himself, fear that his trip to California was in jeopardy. His promise to take care of me revealed an emotion I'd never heard from Jay. He expressed it many times during the weeks that followed.

Of course, we postponed our trip. I changed our plane tickets to the end of the month, three weeks away. Shaken to my core, I wasn't sure how I'd handle the trip. I felt like I needed a village to take care of me, to keep me safe. But Jay gave me a sense of purpose. I didn't want to let him down.

We flew to San Francisco again, but this time I made reservations at the Ritz in Half Moon Bay, certain George was looking down, thinking, "What in the world is she doing? Good Lord, the Ritz?"

Or maybe he was guiding me, as I felt his presence in every part of my being. I knew I needed to be looked after, cared for, and while Jay in his own dear way was as thoughtful and gentle as he could be, I knew we'd both be safe at that hotel.

Steve and Mary were wonderful. They made meals, drove us to the aquarium in Monterey and offered open sympathetic ears. When we left Half Moon Bay for San Francisco, though, we were on our own. After lunch at Fishermen's Wharf, we boarded the boat for Alcatraz, a terrible choice. The coldness of the prison, with real inmate sounds coming through our headsets, was frightening. The clank of barred doors slamming, the rattle of keys and the deafening shouts of prisoners brought us right into the world of incarceration.

When the tour was half over, I asked Jay if he wanted to leave. He quickly said yes. When we got on the boat, I asked why he was so eager. He replied, "Because this is a scary, bad place."

I didn't expect my own reaction to Alcatraz to be so fierce, didn't realize my fragile state would have such an impact on my reactions. Nor did I realize Jay would grasp what the prison was all about. We were both happy to get back to the mainland and to the airport hotel that night. My boy had taken good care of me.

Home meant an empty house. My partner, my best friend, my dearest George would not be there to greet me after this year's trip. Though friends and family rallied around, I was on my own to search for inner peace. It didn't come easily.

That summer on the Cape, as a bunch of kids swam off the dock next door, laughing and shouting with each splash, I wondered if I'd ever feel joyful again. But time *is* a healer, and little by little it began to happen. I started to laugh more and cry less. I never turned down an invitation to dinner or a movie. Jay visited often as did his sisters and their families.

Golf was hard for me though. A long time passed before I could return to our local course, an even longer time before I could play the seventh hole without crying. Now when I climb that hill, I talk to George. I blame him for my bad tee shots and credit him with the good ones. I will carry him in my heart forever.

As summer faded into fall, Pat and I talked a lot about the fact that family dynamics change, and we agreed that a group home might offer Jay more permanent security. It was the next natural step for more independent living.

The Groden Network had received a federal grant from the Department of Housing and Urban Development. Plans were in place to build a new living facility for six special needs adults, and Jay was in line for a space. He didn't like the idea of a group home, probably because of the failed attempt many years before. We discussed it, and I took him to see the house when it was completed. It was new, immaculate, and to Jay's delight, had central air. The one-story house had two wings, each with three bedrooms and a bath, and a central area with a spacious living room, dining room and kitchen. Jay agreed to give it a try. In February 2007, he moved in.

The other residents were higher functioning than Jay, with a variety of physical and developmental disabilities. I worried about how Jay would fit in, how he would handle sharing a bathroom, and sharing responsibility for cooking and cleaning. COVE staff guided the early weeks of his residency, smoothing the transition. Jay was distinctly satisfied with his new home.

But death invaded again. Less than two years after George died, Hedi lost her battle with cancer, and Jay lost his stepmother. He became hyper-aware of his own health. "I am healthy," he repeated. "My mom and my dad are healthy."

Jay instigated a health regimen, doing sit-ups and push-ups daily, walking on the treadmill and riding the stationary bike. He increased his caloric intake with daily milkshakes and became less rigid about second helpings. My skinny guy took on the shape of a well-developed man, with great muscles from marine-style pushups. His weight went up to one-hundred-fifty, and his waist grew to a whopping thirty-two inches.

Jay quickly came to love his house and to genuinely like his housemates. One of the other young men also attends COVE, and they often wait together for the morning bus, talking about things they like. His friend talks about horror movies. Jay tells him about songs on the radio, who the artists are and what year they came out.

Jay's emotional and social growth since he moved into the house is remarkable. More apt to initiate conversation than ever before, he makes his own breakfast, milkshakes and other kinds of food. He has learned communication and socialization skills from his housemates, and he's taught them tidiness and good hygiene in return.

He has also shared his expertise with relaxation therapy with his housemates, often leading daily therapy sessions for both residents and staff. On our way home from a recent trip he remarked, "It is nice to get home again." His house truly has become his home, his anchor in the larger community.

Sometimes Jay astonishes me. When I met him at the bus from Providence one Friday, he asked, "When I die should I have my ashes spread or be buried?"

Without overreacting (or driving off the road), I replied, "Which would you prefer?"

Decisive and calm, he answered, "I would like to have my ashes spread in Bristol and Chatham." With a big grin he added, "I will go to cylinder heaven. I will be 91 when I die." He smiled, having come to terms with a terrible fear.

"Who did you talk to about this, Jay?"

"I did talk to Roland," he responded, his house manager.

Jay also has wonderful conversations with his friend, Mort Dean. Mort was a childhood friend of George's, and we started seeing each other during the summer of 2007. Mort engages Jay in conversation, listens carefully to his interests, and asks related questions.

Once while riding in the car, Mort and Jay were playing a word game of opposites. Mort said a word and asked Jay to respond with a word of the opposite meaning.

"Hot," Mort said. "Cold," Jay responded

"Happy," Mort said. "Sad," Jay said back.

Wide/narrow, big/small, the game went on. Then Mort said "Love." Jay paused for a moment then responded with the steady, serious concentration he gave to the game, "Divorce."

Wow! He hadn't missed a beat all those years ago. When conversations are initiated for him, he often reveals thoughts hidden just below the surface.

Jay is also learning to joke with Mort. Recently having stacked wood for us, he asked Mort how much he thought I would pay him.

Mort answered, "Probably five or six thousand dollars."

Jay stopped, thought for a second and responded, "Huh, good one, Mort."

In December 2009, Jay celebrated his 40th birthday. I asked if he wanted a party. "No thank you," he replied. "I would like to go to Chicago with Mummy and my friend, Mort."

"Why Chicago?" I asked.

"Because I want to go up the Sears Tower and see a view."

The three of us landed at O'Hare Airport at noon and by three o'clock we were at the top of the Sears Tower. We had our picture taken in a Plexiglas cube hanging over the city. Walking from one end of the city to the other, we visited the aquarium and the planetarium, and had dinner atop the John Hancock building.

"This is not my 20th annual trip," Jay assured us. "This is my special 40th birthday trip. I want to go to Mexico again next year."

And so in April 2010, Jay and I again went to Mexico to visit my brother. While we were walking in an open-air market, a young American approached us, said he was a Christian missionary, and asked if he could pray with Jay.

"Be my guest," I said, "but I'm not sure he'll have any idea how to respond."

The missionary put his hand on Jay's shoulder and began to pray. Jay closed his eyes tightly, crossing his fingers, his arms and his legs.

Whether with a missionary or alone with crossed fingers, arms and legs, Jay has let some concept of God into his heart. He is a wonderful son and brother, a gentle uncle, a productive young man who contributes greatly to his world. He just happens to have autism. This isn't the end of his story. It's the beginning of an adult life unfolding with incredible grace.

The staff members at Jay's house tell me that Jay is their star, that they would love a houseful of Jays. Jay is my star, too. And if you ask him how things are going, he'll probably reply, "Two thumbs up! So far, so great!"

LESSON 30

Growing and learning never stop. Jay is the proof.

If I could snap my fingers and be non-autistic,
I would not – because then I wouldn't be me.
Autism is a part of who I am.
TEMPLE GRANDIN

Ultimate Victory

Victory does not imply a "cure" for autism. It means we won over the monsters of fear, guilt, anger and despair. We broke down the ramparts of ignorance and the barriers to effective services. We beat autism by embracing it.

Our journey was long and tough. At times I was lost in a maelstrom of roadblocks, defeated by achingly slow progress and profound isolation. But as the story unfolded, lessons emerged, lessons which helped me over many hurdles, enabling me to define goals and recognize success.

The success is now clear. It can be seen in Jay's everyday life. When I ask him what it means to have autism, it takes him a while to answer because he still finds abstract questions difficult. But when he answers, he uses the word "special." He defines it as what he is able and unable to do. When a friend came by with her twenty-four year old autistic son who does not speak, the two young men who had never met examined each other closely – "in your face" closely. When our guests left, Jay said, "Alexander is autistic."

I asked him what made him say that. He replied, "Because he does not drive a car."

Jay has established his own indicators.

Jay mostly concentrates on what he *can* do. He travels by bus independently. He cooks, cleans and takes meticulous care of his belongings and himself. He works two part-time jobs, and works out daily at a nearby gym. Now he plans to fly to Arizona by himself to visit Mort and me at our winter rental. He truly has spread his wings. This is our victory.

Acknowledgments

Writing a memoir is not an exercise undertaken alone. Many people have contributed and to all of them I am incredibly grateful.

Writer and friend Joan Anderson embraced my initial ideas and offered guidance and encouragement as I struggled with the early chapters. Rose Connors, my editor, the ultimate wordsmith, guided me through the editorial process with impeccable attention to detail and nuance. In addition she managed the publishing of my book along with her business partner Shareen Davis, the cover designer.

Dr. June Groden provided a program of excellent educational and therapeutic services for Jay through the Groden Network. June has devoted her life to the treatment of people with autism and shared her own memories of Jay as a youngster. Pat Fiske, an administrator with the Groden Network, offered a Professional Family Living Arrangement in her home for Jay, a transition to a group home. Jay was with Pat and her husband and daughters for eleven years. They became an extension of our family.

My daughters, Betsy and Allison, patiently read multiple early iterations adding their own memories and perspectives on life with their autistic brother, sharing their emotions and inspiring me to keep going.

Mort Dean, my partner of many years, was my absolute rock, shoring me up when I was at my lowest and guiding me with the wisdom of a true journalist.

I am also grateful to all those families who have taken a similar journey. I listen to so many of their stories and feel their frustration and joy as they trek down a difficult path. They have reassured me that this tale indeed needs to be told.

And Jay, my ultimate inspiration, daily reinforces the importance of communicating our story to a greater audience.